# My Family, My Self

# My Family, My Self

The Latino Guide to Emotional Well-Being

## Mi Familia y Yo

Guía Latina de Bienestar Emocional

Staff from Comunidades Latinas Unidas En Servicio (CLUES)

HAZELDEN

Hazelden
Center City, Minnesota 55012
hazelden.org

ISBN: 978-1-61649-532-9 (pbk); 9-1-61649-529-9 (ebook)
Library of Congress Cataloging-in-Publication Data is on file at the Library of Congress.

Editor's notes:
Most names, details, and circumstances have been changed to protect the privacy of those
mentioned in this publication.

This publication is not intended as a substitute for the advice of health care professionals.

Alcoholics Anonymous and AA are registered trademarks of Alcoholics Anonymous
World Services, Inc.

Appendix: The 40 Developmental Assets® copyright Search Institute, 615 First Avenue NE,
Suite 125, Minneapolis, MN 55413; fax 612-376-8956. Reprinted with permission.

18 17 16 15 14     1 2 3 4 5 6

Cover design: Theresa Jaeger Gedig
Interior design and typesetting: Terri Kinne
Developmental editor: Sid Farrar
Spanish translations: Franklin Curbelo, Acentos
Production editor: Mindy Keskinen

# Contents

# Introduction

WE LATINOS BRING TO THE United States rich and diverse cultural values and practices. But one thing we universally share is that we celebrate and rely on our families: our blood, extended, and chosen families. Family members find strength and support in the roles and expectations passed down through many generations. As individuals, we develop a sense of personal identity and meaning within our families. As we grow older, we find our place within our communities and look forward to contributing to a better world for the coming generations. Throughout our lives, family can provide a safe haven for us as we negotiate the sometimes fast-paced, competitive U.S. culture, with its emphasis on the "rugged individual"—a marked contrast to the value we place on the protecting family. Our sense of well-being within the family serves as a protective blanket as we face language barriers, and different attitudes toward personal issues such as dating and relationships, alcohol and drug use, parenting, and the role of elders. The differences we encounter can cause conflict and confusion and threaten the stability of family life.

For more than thirty years, the professionals at CLUES (Communidades Latinas Unidas En Servicio) have worked with Latinos and their families to provide support and guidance in navigating the psychological, social, and cultural challenges they face in adapting to their new environment. CLUES is a nationally recognized organization based in the Twin Cities of Minneapolis and St. Paul, Minnesota. Our mission is to advance the capacity of Latino families to be healthy, prosperous, and engaged in their communities. We provide services in the areas of health and family well-being, educational achievement, economic vitality, and cultural and civic engagement.

Our approach is holistic. People come to us with a variety of needs and opportunities, but our encounters always convey this question: "What are your hopes and dreams for your future?" This is a sign of our respect for each individual as a whole person, rather than as a set of "problems" to be treated. And it is an expression of our Latino values of *personalismo, respeto,* and hard work to help people find their paths toward their hopes and dreams. It is not surprising that, for most of them, family is in some way a part of who they are and why they have hopes and dreams in the first place. With that as an entry point, we help our clients find many opportunities to improve their well-being.

Our clients inspire us with their love, kindness, resilience, and faith in the future. With this book, we hope to share a few of the lessons they've taught us during the past thirty years. This book consists of seven chapters, each focused on a topic that we have found relevant to most of our clients at some point in their lives. Attention to these seven areas will help a person and family fulfill some of their hopes and dreams.

- *Chapter 1: Who Am I?* focuses on the challenging topic of personal identity. In the United States, we Latinos face many issues regarding identity. First, we are often labeled as *foreign* or *a minority* by the dominant culture. Then, of course, there is the socially constructed ethnic identity of being *Latino,* even though most of us identify more with a particular neighborhood or region in a country. Furthermore, there are many other social identities that inform who we are—such as our sex, gender, sexual orientation, specific religious affiliation (or lack of it), social class, and body ability or disability. Most important, we have our core individual identities, nested in our larger sense of family and community. This chapter explores the forces that shape identity and the ways we can harmonize them by deepening our personal understanding of identity.

- *Chapter 2: Family* explores one of two key values shared by almost all Latinos, the sense of well-being that comes from our family. (The other universal key value, spirituality, is addressed in chapter 7.) In this chapter, we discuss different types of families, some basic parenting skills, and the critical role of elders in our lives. We consider the ways in which immigration and acculturation change our traditional roles, and the tragedy of violence in the home. The information and skills discussed here can help families find greater happiness through understanding our different needs and roles in supporting each other while we find our own places in the community and the world.

- *Chapter 3: Emotions in Harmony* is an introduction to what emotions are and how they shape our experiences. Many Latinos have experienced intense, unfortunate events during immigration, and others have faced difficult times before and after immigration as well. This chapter helps us understand some of these traumatic experiences, the benefits of visiting a counselor, how emotional events can complicate relationships, and how we can care for our emotions.

- *Chapter 4: With My Feet on the Ground* discusses alcohol, other drugs, and the risk of addiction. In this chapter, we describe how these substances affect the body and brain and what parents can do to help their children avoid risky behaviors that can lead to early substance use. We discuss patterns in Latino families that protect us and those that put us at risk, what alcoholism and drug addiction are, how addictions can be treated, and how family can be part of treatment and recovery.

- *Chapter 5: Making a Living* is about the important role of financial stability in finding mental health. Our financial well-being influences our sense of security and self-esteem, and it is a driving force for many other choices we make. In this chapter, we cover topics important to financial stability in the United States, including getting an education, developing new skills, career planning, and basic financial skills such as budgeting, using credit, and building assets.

- *Chapter 6: In a Foreign Country* is especially written for first-generation immigrants, although the children of these immigrants will also benefit from this chapter. We review some of the traumatic events related to immigration and adjustment, strategies that have helped many Latinos adapt to life as a "foreigner" in their new home, how discrimination and crime affect us, and some ideas on what it means to be bicultural.

- *Chapter 7: Drawing Strength and Joy from Our Spiritual Life* is about the feeling of transcendence that most Latinos share, which is a valuable component of our well-being. We review our shared religious history. We look at how spirituality helps us cope with issues of *acculturation*—adjusting to another culture—and helps us through difficult times. In our new home, our children and grandchildren meet and marry many people from other cultures and religious/spiritual experiences. We explore how to negotiate differences in spirituality and religion within the family so that we can maintain harmony.

At the end of each chapter, you will find a summary and reflection questions to help you think about the information in that chapter. You will also find a summary of each chapter in Spanish with selected reflection questions. These can be shared and discussed with family members who don't read English. There are many personal stories within this book. Please understand that we have seen thousands of clients. The stories you read here are all "true" in that they represent the experiences of actual Latinos. However, they also contain some fiction, since some of them have been composed by combining many stories into one. Details have been changed, and any resemblance to a real person is strictly coincidental. These stories were created to help you understand how the issues we're discussing affect people's lives.

All readers, but especially dominant-culture readers and counselors, should note that *everything* in this book is a generalization. We doubt you will find any one Latino or Latina who can relate to every single issue discussed here. At the same time, experience tells us that *something* in this book will apply to every reader. Every encounter at CLUES involves the personal question "What are your hopes and dreams for your future?" In the same way, every reader and every counselor needs to absorb this information with attention to his or her unique concerns, needs, and hopes. Every person is different. This book is not a substitute for services provided by skilled practitioners in the seven areas discussed. In fact, our hope is that it will inspire readers to find providers for similar services and to seek help before issues become overwhelming.

We hope this book is a help to you! Should you wish to learn more about CLUES, you may visit us online at www.clues.org.

## Summary: Introduction

We Latinos bring to the United States rich and diverse cultural values and practices. But one thing we universally share is that we celebrate and rely on our family. Family members find strength and support in the roles and expectations passed down through many generations. As individuals, we develop a sense of personal identity and meaning within the family. As we grow older, we find our place within our communities and look forward to contributing to a better world for the coming generations. Throughout our lives, family can provide a safe haven for us as we negotiate the sometimes fast-paced, competitive U.S. culture, with its emphasis on the "rugged individual"—a marked contrast to our value of the protecting family. Our sense of well-being within the family serves as a protective blanket as we face language barriers, different attitudes toward personal issues such as dating and relationships, alcohol and drug use, parenting, and the role of elders. The differences we encounter can cause conflict and confusion and threaten the stability of family life.

The authors of this book are staff members at Comunidades Latinas Unidas En Servicio, a nationally recognized organization based in the Twin Cities of Minneapolis and St. Paul, Minnesota. Our mission at CLUES is to advance the capacity of Latino families to be healthy, prosperous, and engaged in their communities. We provide services in the areas of health and family well-being, educational achievement, economic vitality, and cultural and civic engagement.

Our encounters begin with this question: "What are your hopes and dreams for your future?" This question expresses our Latino values of *personalismo, respeto,* and hard work to help people find their paths toward their hopes and dreams. With the importance of family as an entry point, we help our clients find many opportunities to improve their well-being.

With this book, we hope to share a few of the lessons they've taught us during the past thirty years. Note: A Spanish-language version of each chapter summary appears at the end of each chapter. These translations can be used to introduce these ideas to family members who don't read English, and to spark discussion. A set of "reflection questions" is also included at the end of each chapter.

## Resumen: Introducción

Nosotros como latinos traemos a los Estados Unidos costumbres y valores culturales muy ricos y variados. Pero hay algo que todos nosotros tenemos en común que es celebrar y depender en nuestra familia. Los familiares encuentran fortaleza y apoyo en los roles y expectativas transmitidas a través de muchas generaciones. Como individuos, desarrollamos un sentido de identidad personal y significado dentro de la familia. A medida que envejecemos, encontramos un lugar propio dentro de nuestras comunidades, y estamos deseosos de aportar esfuerzos para dejar un mundo mejor para las generaciones venideras. Durante nuestras vidas, la familia nos brinda un refugio seguro para lidiar con la cultura competitiva y veloz de los Estados Unidos, que enfatiza la cualidad de "individuo independiente" *(rugged individual)*—que es un contraste bien marcado con nuestro valor de la familia protectora. Nuestro sentimiento de bienestar dentro de la familia sirve de escudo protector cuando enfrentamos barreras del idioma, y actitudes diferentes acerca de temas personales como por ejemplo: salir en pareja y las relaciones, consumo de alcohol y drogas, ser padre y el rol de los ancianos. Las diferencias que encontramos pueden causar conflicto, confusión y amenazan la estabilidad de la vida familiar.

Los escritores de este libro son empleados de Comunidades Latinas Unidas En Servicio, una organización reconocida a nivel nacional, con sede en las Ciudades Gemelas de Minneapolis y St. Paul, Minnesota. Nuestra misión es avanzar la capacidad de las familias latinas a ser más saludables, prósperas e involucradas en sus comunidades. Ofrecemos servicios en las áreas de salud comunitaria, bienestar familiar, éxito académico, potencial económico, y participación cultural y cívica.

Nuestros encuentros comienzan con esta pregunta: "¿Cuáles son las esperanzas y sueños para tu futuro?" Esta pregunta expresa nuestros valores de *personalismo, respeto,* y trabajar con empeño para ayudar a las personas a encontrar su camino para la realización de sus esperanzas y sueños. Tomando como punto inicial la importancia de la familia, ayudamos a nuestros clientes a encontrar muchas oportunidades para mejorar su bienestar.

Con este libro esperamos compartir algunas lecciones que nuestros clientes nos han enseñado en los últimos treinta años.

CHAPTER

···one···

# Who Am I?

## At a Glance

Chapter 1 is about *identity,* our personal sense of self. Each of us has a unique identity, but it is shaped by many things, including our family and our culture. In this chapter you will learn:

- what we mean by "identity" and why it is important to mental health
- some ways to think about what the label "Latino" means in the United States
- some common elements of identity shared by most Latinos
- how identity helps with mental health and creates some risk factors as well
- how we can gain control of our personal sense of identity

WHEN YOU ARE TRAVELING, it helps to have a destination and a way to ask for directions. In the journey of life, most of us have a vague sense of where we want to go. We want happiness and health for the people we care about—our families, our friends, our community—and for ourselves. But our life journey is complicated, and a map and some directions would certainly ease our path. The journey toward health and happiness begins with an understanding of *who we are*. We call this our "identity."

Getting our hands on that map and getting some directions helps us when we run into obstacles. We all need that map from time to time. With the map in hand, we are also better able to ask for directions when we need help.

Of course, every person is different, and every person has a different map. But all geographical maps share some common features, for example, mountains, valleys, lakes, deserts, plains, rivers, and oceans. "People maps" also share some features. This chapter will help you understand some of those features.

### The meaning of identity

What do we mean by identity? As an example, let's look at the story of Oliverio, who was raised in Mexico, then immigrated to the United States.

As a young man, Oliverio was energetic, handsome, a weight lifter and exercise fanatic, and a very hard worker. He took a variety of jobs, most them involving hard physical labor, which he enjoyed. Because of his strength and endurance, he made good money. In his mid-thirties, he was unmarried and often helped his mother, grandparents, and younger siblings by sending money home to the family.

Oliverio had become a hard worker at an early age. He and his siblings were raised by his grandfather, who passed away when Oliverio was fourteen. As the oldest of six children, Oliverio found work to help feed the family. His natural athletic talents helped him do well, and he left school to get a better job and be the man of the house. As his younger siblings got older, they began to help too. Finally, when he was twenty, he heard about a good job in the United States and left his home in Mexico. He made good money and sent a lot of it home. He loved calling his family and was especially proud when his younger brothers and sisters asked him for advice and told him about their lives and dreams.

Oliverio had been here more than ten years and had just decided it was time to settle down when he suffered a devastating physical injury. He could no longer lift the weights that had made him so valuable to employers, so he found light-duty work.

Soon, Oliverio began to lose pride in himself. With lower wages and many medical bills, he could not send as much money to his mother, although he usually found a way to send something. He could not contribute to savings for his younger siblings. He could not give money to his church. He could not buy his friends drinks at the cantina.

Oliverio went from feeling confident about asking women out and being ready to start his own family to feeling bashful. He felt he was less of a man. He felt he did not look good. He did not want to hang out with his friends. Their stories about dates with women left him feeling sad, and he couldn't buy the first round of beer. Even when he wanted to ask a woman out, he felt he could no longer afford to show what a good partner he was. His picture of who he was and what he was good at had changed. He became sad and depressed.

Oliverio's story raises some interesting questions about identity:

- Was Oliverio a different person after his injury?
- How much of our personal identity is tied to the things we do? How much comes from something else inside us?
- How is our self-respect related to how we think other people see us?
- How could Oliverio's sense of identity be used to overcome his current challenges?

These questions all relate to our sense of *identity*. Identity shapes our mental health and well-being. As Latinos in the United States, we are perhaps more deeply aware of the idea of identity because we have had a variety of labels forced on us. People here may describe us as Latino, Hispanic, Chicano, Mexican-American, Puerto Rican, and many other labels. "Latino" is an identity that someone else applies to us. But it is only one part of our identity. In fact, it is just one of our identities.

We may think of ourselves as one person who is always the same. But Oliverio's story shows that Oliverio's identity was a land with many features. Before his accident, Oliverio identified as

- an economic and social contributor to his family, siblings, and church
- an athlete and a hard worker who was sought by employers
- a person who always paid his debts and somehow found extra to share with his friends
- a man who was attractive to women and looking forward to starting his own family

In daily life, we all have *many* identities. We use them as we relate to different people and to different groups. These identities are fluid; they can change over time.

An identity that has been very helpful in one setting can become a drawback in another. For example, part of Oliverio's identity was as a physically strong provider, a leader who always did a little better than the others and could help them out. After his injury, he could not fulfill those expectations using the same methods he once had.

Our identity affects how we feel about ourselves, especially when something happens that challenges or changes our picture of who we are. You could say that with the loss of his physical strength, Oliverio had lost a close friend and was in grief over that loss.

It is helpful to think of identity as *many* parts rather than one thing. Some people describe this as having many T-shirts, each with a different picture and slogan on it. We wear them all at once, but only show one or two at a time. Or, we may think of ourselves as being like a mosaic made of many tiles, which we reveal as they are needed. In this chapter we have described identity as being like a map with many features on it. Regardless of which mental model "fits" us, knowing our personal identity can help us manage our life journey. Being aware of the unique features of our identity and feeling satisfied with them will help us make choices that are healthy and right for us. When we are unhappy about certain aspects of our identity, we can explore the possibility of changing them, or we can learn to accept them and turn them into something positive.

We all have many features to our identity, but we only show certain features to certain people. We are usually unaware that we are doing this. Take a moment to think about how you behave with your family, with your close friends, with new people you meet, when you are at church, when you are with someone to whom you are romantically attracted, and when you are alone. Most of us reveal ourselves as a slightly different person in each of these settings.

Just as maps of the land share certain features, maps of identity share some features. Counselors say that, for most people, our identity maps include these basic features:

1. *Race:* a category defined mostly by physical traits that relate to the geographic region your ancestors came from. It is important to note that these categories are usually socially defined and do not have a biological basis—scientists do not recognize different "races" of human beings. But the social reality *does* affect how we are identified. In the United States, officially recognized races include White, American Indian and Alaska Native, Asian, Black or African American, Native Hawaiian and Other Pacific Islander, and Two or More Races.[1]

2. *Ethnic and national identity:* the cultural heritage with which you identify. Many factors make up a shared culture, including ancestry, history, homeland, language, religion, cuisine, style of dress, and even physical appearance.

3. *Ability/disability:* the skills and challenges that affect your life in the community. These include physical, cognitive, mental, sensory, emotional, and developmental abilities or disabilities. We are born with some of these, and others can be acquired over time.

4. *Religious affiliation or spirituality:* how or whether you were raised in a religion, and whether you identify with a religion now. This category also includes the sense of "transcendence," which may be described as a belief that there is more to the universe than what we can perceive with our senses and through rational exploration.

5. *Class:* your social status (and the social status of your peers) relative to other groups.

6. *Sex:* whether you have the physical equipment to be female or male.

7. *Gender:* whether you identify more with characteristically male or female behaviors as defined by your culture. (Some people may be physically male but identify with cultural female role expectations, for example, or be physically female but identify with behaviors culturally perceived as male.)

**8.** *Sexual orientation:* a category based on the sex/gender of the people to whom you are most romantically/sexually attracted.

We have many ways of talking about these parts of the identity map, and some people would include more or fewer basic features, but we have found these eight categories useful. Different cultures define the categories differently. For example, in the United States, "class" usually refers to an economic status: how much money your household earns indicates your status as upper class, middle class, or lower class. But in much of Latin America, class is more related to a person's ancestry, meaning the social class of their parents, as well as their degree of education, their occupation, and in some countries, their skin color.

Some of the features on the identity map are inborn and/or unchangeable: whether we are born male or female, our height and skin color, where we were raised, and who our ancestors were. Some features on the map change over time. For example, Oliverio's identity changed in regard to ability/disability as a result of his injury. In his new home, his economic class also changed, because his reduced income meant he was no longer middle class.

### Being "Latino"

The term "Latino" is an inclusive one that refers to our geographic roots in Latin America. We may have come from Latin America ourselves, or we may be descended from immigrants. Or perhaps our ancestors didn't actually "immigrate"; they already lived in Spanish-colonized areas (such as today's New Mexico) that later became part of the United States. But whichever is true for us, our ethnicity is probably a very important aspect of our identity.

"Latino" only makes sense if you are not from Latin America and need some label to put on people who come from there. Latin America is *huge,* and the reality is that we are quite diverse. Some of us descend directly from the indigenous people who were here before European settlement. Some come from Asia, some from Africa, some from northern Europe, and many have mixed heritage. Some of us speak only Spanish, some Portuguese, some an indigenous tongue. It is odd to arrive in the United States seeing ourselves as one thing and be called another.

We may identify as Colombian or Honduran, but here, the dominant culture puts a label on us. Usually we are referred to as "Latino" or "Hispanic." We at CLUES prefer the term "Latino" because it is more inclusive, referring to our shared geographic history of Latin America. "Hispanic" tends to exclude those of us who are not Spanish speakers.

The first point all readers of this book—Latino or other—must understand is that every individual must be understood on his or her own terms. Country of origin, family of origin, ancestry, history, economic conditions, political status, social status, and other facts shape the particular identity of any individual. This is why, when we get to know each other, we must discard preconceived notions about whom other people are and simply ask questions instead.

However, it may be generally said that many Latinos do share some elements of identity: a sense of self, *familismo*, traditional roles, *personalismo, simpatía, machismo, respeto,* and religion and spirituality.

### Sense of self

We Latinos tend to understand who we are based on the role we play in a group and how others judge us. We see ourselves as part of a group—an extended family—and we derive our sense of pride not just from our own achievements but from those of our group.

For example, whether from Guatemala or Argentina, a Latina mother is going to derive much of her satisfaction from how well her children, nieces and nephews, and other family members do in their lives. Although this is true for many American mothers, it is more likely to be true for Latinas.

Or for example, we take enormous pride when the soccer team from our country of origin succeeds or when someone from our country of origin becomes famous or succeeds in politics.

As compared to the dominant culture here, we derive more personal benefit from our sense of how our group is doing. This group sense of self is called "collectivism," meaning that we think of our identity in reference to the successes of others who are important to us. In contrast, the U.S. culture is more individualistic. A person raised in the U.S. culture gains more sense of identity from the person's own accomplishments and setbacks and is less influenced by the status of a group.

## *Familismo*

Closely related to our collectivist sense of self is that we strongly value family and enjoy being connected to a great many people. Family extends beyond immediate blood relationships to include many generations, cousins, godparents, friends, and other affiliated people, even if there is no blood-based connection. Families will bind together to help others with financial need, health issues, work, advice, and other life issues. We believe in supporting our elders, who possess wisdom and deserve our respect, and we enjoy extended, multigenerational households. We express *familismo* through cooperation, by protecting the family honor, and by placing the needs of the family ahead of our own needs. Sharing food is an important way of bonding in the family.[2]

Immigration has placed added stress on the family, as parents and family members are split, some remaining in the country of origin. And, in the United States, adult children are more likely to move far from home—a fact that can cause stress among generations of Latinos.

In the dominant U.S. culture, the sense of family usually includes fewer people, and families tend to be smaller. Our broader definition of "family" can lead to mis-understandings when we are talking to U.S. service providers, health care providers, counselors, teachers, government authorities, and others who are from the dominant culture. They may not understand how very important our extended family is to us. Most Latinos feel distressed when the family becomes separated for an extended period of time. (And remember, for us, "family" includes more people than it does for many people in the dominant culture.) We may feel sad or experience other uncomfortable emotions.

## *Traditional roles*

Typically, men are the head of the house and the breadwinners, while women are homemakers who cook, clean, and raise children. We want to be sure that others see us as doing these jobs well. Children may live with parents until marriage. And it is not unusual for many people from an extended family to live under one roof. Both mother and father work to instill the importance of values, such as honor, good manners, and respect for authority and for elders. Immigration and economic stress add a source of conflict in the family. Many Latinas who once would have been homemakers need to work outside the home, and they may find work more readily than their mate. This can create conflict.

In the U.S. culture, roles are more fluid and less tied to one's gender. Everyone is usually expected to work, unless they can afford not to. Although homemaking is recognized as a form of work, other work that brings in income is afforded more respect.

### Personalismo

Generally, Latinos value having close relationships with relatives and friends. We enjoy sharing food, gatherings, and other rituals that reinforce our sense of belonging to a group. Personal contact is extremely important. We are people-oriented. Personal relationships mean more than status or the pursuit of wealth and advancement.

English does not have a term close to *personalismo,* which indicates that this value is not emphasized in U.S. culture. Some people describe U.S. culture as "transactional." This way of thinking carries the perspective that "if I do something for you, you will do something for me." From a Latino perspective, relationships in the United States involve mutual exchanges but appear less personal.

A Latino who is dealing with a professional from the dominant U.S. culture, such as a counselor or doctor or lawyer, may view the person's neutral or businesslike approach as negative. In our personal and professional relationships, we try to take the time necessary to show our respect, and we expect that others will offer a similar courtesy.[3]

### Simpatía

Latinos tend to favor harmonious relationships over adversarial ones. It is not so much that we want to avoid conflict as that we prefer to see our group operating in harmony. This means that we are less likely to question authority figures and elders and more likely to avoid direct conflict with people in authority. We may agree with something in order to preserve harmony.

### Machismo

The value of *machismo* refers to the expectation that males take responsibility for being providers and for bringing honor to the family. To fulfill his role, a male must be trustworthy, courteous, courageous, wise, and respectful. He must show leadership. The role also includes safeguarding family honor by protecting family secrets.

In U.S. culture, *machismo* has taken on negative connotations of being physically and sexually aggressive. This disregards the positive values and noble behavior that men are encouraged to embrace as part of traditional *machismo*.

### Respeto

*Respeto,* or respect, refers to the way we relate to other people and acknowledge differences in perceived social status. Age, gender, class, and occupation are all indicators of respect due. Latinos generally feel that great respect is due to parents, elders, teachers, doctors, and those with greater education or in positions of authority. Children are to show respect by obeying parental wishes, usually without challenge. In general, it makes the Latino culture more hierarchical.

We Latinos tend to automatically show respect to someone because of their social class or position. For example, we show respect to teachers because they are the authority in the classroom, and we show respect to elders because they are wise. In the United States, respect is not granted so automatically. For example, a U.S. parent is likely to wait for teachers to prove themselves to be knowledgeable. They are more likely to wait for an elder to demonstrate wisdom and other characteristics worthy of respect. In the United States, the idea is that people are due respect when they prove that they are worthy of it.

In interactions with therapists, doctors, and others in authority, Latinos may be less likely to ask questions, perhaps viewing this as a form of disrespect. We may be more formal as a way of showing respect, but this can be interpreted in the U.S. culture as maintaining distance.[4]

### Religion and spirituality

We Latinos tend to have a strong sense of transcendence, no matter whether we have been raised in a religious tradition. That is, most of us believe in a sense of mystery—that the universe is more than what our senses and rational exploration can determine. (We'll explore this idea in chapter 7.)

In the United States, 68 percent of Latinos identify as Roman Catholic, 15 percent identify as Evangelical Protestants, 9 percent identify with other religious groups, and 8 percent do not identify with any religion. Of Latinos who have recently immigrated to the United States, 74 percent are Roman Catholic.[5]

Our "Latino" ethnic identity is artificial because another group has imposed it on us, but it doesn't really fit. Many of us don't simply identify with a country; we identify with a specific region, city, town, or neighborhood. Some of us are indigenous. So in addition to our personally claimed identity, we have this "Latino" identity to contend with.

Let's listen to Esperanza as she describes how this second identity carries both gifts and challenges. She was born in Mexico, where she lived until the age of eighteen. At that time, she moved to the United States to attend college—and she found work and a different life.

▪▪▪ *In Mexico, I didn't have to think about where I was from as part of my identity. I was just me. When I came to the U.S., I found out that people thought of me as Mexican or Latina first, and then got to know who I was second. I'm not just Esperanza. I'm a Mexican, a Latina. So they saw me as representing something else. They had a set of expectations about what I would be like. The way people in the U.S. saw me began to influence how I saw myself.*

*Sometimes the stereotypes are very upsetting. They affect opportunities that are presented to you, such as job prospects. It is strange that the majority culture in the U.S. lumps me in with Colombians and Puerto Ricans. It can make you weary. Especially when people speak slowly and loudly because they think I can't understand them!*

*As an adult, coming to a place where people speak differently, have a different system, and have a different culture can make you feel like a child. You have to learn things an adult should know, like how to take the bus, and how to get medical insurance. These things all operate differently in the U.S. than at home. You see yourself as competent and now you find that you feel incompetent in the new culture.*

*But in time I also began to value the impact of being "other" on my identity. I began to see the strengths in my country of origin. This only came after years of being frustrated by Americans treating me as different. But in this country, part of my identity is as a minority. I have an identity as Esperanza and an identity as representing a culture. This has helped shape my career.*

*It is said that sometimes you don't really begin to learn something until you have to teach it. Part of what I do is teach people who I am, and that includes explaining where I come from. I feel that I actually have a stronger sense of my own identity since I have had the experience of being a Mexican in the U.S.* ▪▪▪

Esperanza is clear about her identity and has drawn strength from it. This is part of the value of answering the question, *¿Quién soy yo?* As we gain perspective on how we define ourselves and how others define us, we gain some measure of control over the shape of our life journey.

### Protective and risk factors in identity

Each person's identity can be a source of strength and a guide to his or her journey. But facets of identity also can make the path more difficult.

Eligio moved to the United States from Colombia about fifteen years ago. He explains that he's always been very conscious of his identity, both here and back in Colombia.

■■■ *In Colombia, I was the son of a well-educated professional couple—a lawyer and a senior accountant. I'm a light-skinned male, and I was part of the upper middle class in Colombia. I experienced many privileges there that I was unaware of, simply because I was white, I was male, my parents were professionals, and I had the opportunity to get a professional degree.*

*I came to the United States to pursue a doctoral degree. I arrived as an experienced professional, respected by my community. But I soon found that I was seen otherwise. My English skills, which were excellent in Colombia, barely sufficed in school. My strong accent labeled me as different. Even though I was white, my Spanish-tinged accent made me a "person of color." I went from being privileged to experiencing prejudice.*

*But there were advantages too. I am a gay man. In Colombia, this is not an acceptable identity, and I had experienced oppression there. Here in the U.S., at least in some areas, it is very acceptable and has even opened doors to new communities of people who are more open-minded. I found mentors and helpers who were from the gay community. So in Colombia, my identity as a gay man was a disadvantage, but here it offered some advantages.*

*Growing up with a sense of entitlement in Colombia made my adjustment to the U.S. interesting. On the one hand, I had to become accustomed to experiencing some prejudice. On the other hand, I had a sense of self-confidence and knew who I was even though other people's labels sometimes made my life more difficult.* ■■■

Regardless of where we are from, we all know that in some situations, some parts of our identity can be helpful and other parts can hold us back. Understanding our identity can help us navigate the challenges we may face—challenges such as being undocumented, alcoholism and addiction, new freedoms, divorce and separation, and traditional roles. Let's examine each of these.

### The condition of being undocumented

Here at CLUES, we see people who have always considered themselves honest, hard-working, and strong of character. They have fled political oppression, the activities of criminals in their home regions, and extreme economic hardship, and they are now undocumented immigrants in the United States without legal papers. For these people, the identity of "undocumented" is challenging in several ways. It is hard to live in fear of another country's authorities, even more so when part of your identity is as someone who respects authority. It is hard to live apart from your family when your family is so much a part of who you are. And it is hard to live outside of the law when you have spent most of your life as a law-abiding person.

These conditions stress the parts of identity that relate to family, honesty and integrity, and maintaining harmony. These conditions may separate husbands, wives, children, and parents. They may mean that children who speak English better than their parents do much of the negotiating for the family, upsetting our sense of respect based on traditional roles. Wives may have an easier time finding work than their husbands, which challenges the roles of women and men.

So if we are in the United States without papers, some of our expectations about who we are can be thwarted, and we feel unhappy as a result. But some aspects of our identity add great strength. For example, our strong extended family can be a great support to us in figuring out how to survive. And our strong sense of being hardworking individuals can help us make contributions to the community we live in.

### Alcoholism and addiction

Some people struggle with addiction to alcohol or to drugs. Sometimes these people begin to see their entire identity as being an alcoholic or a drug addict. Yet a key to their recovery from addiction is the strong, internalized sense of family, even if the actual ties with their families have been severed. Remembering that their behavior affects the rest of their family can help them return to a strong identity, not as an alcoholic or an addict, but as a family member. The solid extended family that is so prevalent in Latino culture can be a great protective asset in recovering from addiction. When we make a change for the better, a strong family support system can help us maintain that change. We have an entire community invested in our success.

### New kinds of freedom

One of the joys of gaining clarity about our personal identity is that we feel a new freedom to explore aspects of identity. In the United States, which emphasizes individual choice and responsibility over collectivism, we may feel much freer to explore identity. However, stepping out of the norm can be hard for us. We may be teased or picked on by members of our community or family who feel threatened when we try something different from the norm. For example, people who are struggling with mental health issues may *have* to try new things to feel better. Here, strong family support and community harmony can, at first, be an impediment to success. Family members may think that when we try something new that we are being weird or that we are betraying our families of origin. But many Latinos have done it anyway. We may find that by talking with our families and explaining that we must try this change to feel better, they gradually accept us. When we stick to our goals even when the family and community resist our decisions, they usually come to respect our change and feel that we were brave to take a new path. Once again, they rally around us. So although the family may hold us back for a time, eventually they embrace the positive changes.

### Divorce and separation

Marital strife challenges personal identity. Family is very important, but not every marriage or relationship will succeed. And living in a new culture adds to marital stress. When a marriage or relationship is troubled, both partners face challenges to their identities that are strongly rooted in our sense of roles.

### Traditional roles

In the United States, our expectations related to traditional gender roles may be challenged. The traditional expectation may be that men make the decisions and women become homemakers, but here, gender roles are much more fluid. A couple from Latin

America who raise their children in the United States may find that their children adopt the dominant culture's ideas about men's and women's roles, which disrupts family harmony. Adult daughters may want to pursue careers instead of having a family. Adult sons may marry and stay home to tend the children. These roles are acceptable in the United States but feel out of place to Latinos who have traditional values.

A traditional Latina mother whose children have grown up in the United States and are influenced by its individualism may face some great challenges when one or more of her children fail to meet her expectations. She gains much of her sense of pride and competence from how well her children do. Their success reflects directly on who she is. A U.S.-born mother cares deeply about her children, too, but she is not as likely to see her children's failures as a threat to her own competence. Our personal story, our identity, helps shape the choices we make and the opportunities we pursue. If you believe, for example, that you are good at persuading people, that belief becomes part of your identity. Success in that area affirms your belief. You are likely to pursue activities that you will be successful at.

### Gaining control of identity

Let's return to Oliverio's story. Oliverio finally sought help from a counselor for his problems, because he was so sad. The counselor saw many other things that Oliverio was ignoring about himself. The counselor saw a man who cared a lot about his family, who had made his way in the world, who was very skilled at persuading, and who understood a lot about physical strength, healthy diet, and how to work hard. The counselor saw a man of great integrity—for example, finding a way to pay for medical bills when he was uninsured. The counselor saw a man who once had been a model to others, so he knew what it felt like to take responsibility for helping other people. Although Oliverio no longer had physical strength as an asset, he still possessed these other experiences and other identities.

Oliverio's picture of himself—his identity—had been shattered by his injury. The injury had disrupted his map of who he was. That was his struggle—to find his place on the identity map again, perhaps even to draw a new map. The counselor helped Oliverio with this map. Oliverio regained faith in his competencies as a person. He found ways to use his skills in the community, with his friends, as a man, and with his family.

Oliverio is now identifying other talents and personality assets that do not rely on his physical strength. He had been afraid to tell too much to his family at home about his injury for fear of worrying them, but he has now told them, and they are providing their emotional support as he works to find a new path. He has learned that his younger siblings and some of his friends still look up to him, even though he doesn't have the strength or earning capacity that once gave him pride. Instead of isolating himself from his friends because he couldn't be the guy who bought everyone a round of drinks, he is seeing them again and finding strength in their friendships.

Oliverio's journey is not complete, and he is still developing his new map. He is exploring, and his story will continue. As he strikes out in new directions, he will learn about other strengths and skills. He once had one set of answers to the question, *¿Quién soy yo?* Now he is developing another set of answers. This is not an easy task. He is gaining greater control over his identity, and this will give him better control over the shape of his journey. It means that the next time he suffers a setback, he will have new skills to regain his way.

We Latinos find ourselves contending with the different expectations of the dominant culture every day. What can we do when we have to live with circumstances that don't fit well with our identity?

- Acknowledge that the uncomfortable feelings are based on this discrepancy.
- Remember that the idea of who we are is flexible and can change with life experiences.
- Search for the positive parts of ourselves that are harmonious with our new circumstances.
- Explore those aspects of the new circumstances that are under our control and decide whether we want to change them.
- Look for support in our community, especially with someone who experienced a similar struggle and has overcome it.
- Allow ourselves to be helped, including seeking professional counseling, therapy, or a support group.

## Summary: Chapter 1—Who Am I?

This book begins with the subject of *identity* because understanding identity is one of the keys to mental health. Each person has their own identity, constructed of individual experiences and attribute, but it develops in the context of the expectations of our family and culture. Most Latinos share a *collective* identity, meaning that we draw our sense of who we are from the group to which we belong. Some of the important elements of our identity include shared values around family, feelings of spirituality, *respeto*, *personalismo*, and other elements. In contrast, the dominant culture in the U.S. is more individualist. One of the interesting aspects of identity is that here in the U.S., we are collectively labeled as "Latino" even though we see ourselves as being from a certain region or even neighborhood.

Our identity can be a source of great strength, but our mental health can be at risk when something happens that shatters our sense of identity. Learning to understand the features of our identity can help us find ways to live happy lives.

### Reflection questions

The "reflection questions" found throughout this book offer ideas for thought and conversation.

1. If somebody asks me who I am, what do I say about myself?

2. Do I tell the same thing to everybody? Do I tell myself something different than what I tell other people?

3. Where does my identity come from—the stories I tell myself about who I am? How did I form these ideas about myself?

4. Am I happy with my identity? What do I like? What would you like to change? How?

5. What are some difficulties with trying to change?

6. What are some things about my identity that I cannot change? Why? What prevents me from making those changes?

7. If I came from a different country than where I live now, how does the story about myself change?

**Resumen: Capítulo 1—¿Quién soy yo?**

Este libro comienza con el tema de *identidad,* dado que entender el sentido de quienes somos es clave para nuestra salud mental. Para cada uno de nosotros, nuestra identidad proviene de nuestras experiencias y atributos, pero se desarrolla dentro de las expectativas de nuestra familia y cultura. La mayoría de los latinos comparten una identidad colectiva: obtenemos nuestro sentido de quienes somos del grupo al que pertenecemos. Nuestra indentidad incluye valores compartidos de la familia, sentimientos de espiritualidad, *respeto, personalismo,* y otros elementos. En contraste, la cultura dominante de los Estados Unidos es más individualística. Un aspecto interesante de la identidad es que en los Estados Unidos, se nos pone la etiqueta de "latino", aun cuando nos vemos a nosotros mismos como seres de una región o incluso de un vecindario en particular.

Nuestra identidad es una fuente de gran fortaleza, pero nuestra salud mental puede correr riesgo cuando sucede algo que destruye nuestro sentido de identidad. Aprender a comprender las características de nuestra identidad nos puede ayudar a encontrar formas de vivir felices

Preguntas para reflexionar:

- ¿De dónde proviene mi identidad—las cosas que me digo a mismo sobre quién soy?
- ¿Cómo me formé estas ideas sobre mi mismo?
- ¿Estoy feliz con mi identidad? ¿Qué me agrada, y qué me gustaría cambiar? ¿Cómo?

CHAPTER

···two···

# Family

Chapter 2 is about **family.** Harmony with our family affects our mental well-being. In this chapter, we will learn about how the meaning of family varies from one person to another and about how important our concept of family is in our lives. Some of the topics we will cover include these:

- healthy traditions of Latino families
- dating and intercultural relationships
- parenting skills
- family communication skills
- positive ways to maintain discipline
- how to help your children do well in school
- respecting and caring for our elders
- the impact of immigration and acculturation
- child abuse and domestic violence

WHEN WE WERE PREPARING TO write this chapter, we gathered a number of our Latino elders together and asked them a tough question: "You are going to leave for a desert island. You can bring only a few things with you. These things must represent what you love best about your culture. What do you choose to bring?"

We had a very fun conversation. Many answers came up, but two ideas were repeated again and again: our love of God and our love of family. The themes of *family* and *spirituality* are important to most Latinos. We will discuss spirituality in chapter 7. In this chapter, we will learn about family:

- what we mean by "family"
- healthy traditions of Latino families
- dating and intercultural relationships
- parenting skills
- family communication skills
- positive ways to maintain discipline
- how to help your children do well in school
- respecting and caring for our elders
- the impact of immigration and acculturation
- child abuse and domestic violence

### What is a family?

This question seems simple, but is it? If we think about the families we know, Latino and non-Latino, we see many different answers to this question. Family consists of many things:

- love between two people
- connections that include blood ties, friendship, a sense of loyalty, a sense of obligation, and a sense of mutual help

- joy shared among people who care about each other
- people legally bound to care for each other

The elders we spoke with had many kinds of families. Some might be considered traditional families, which included a mother and father, children and their spouses, grandchildren, boyfriends and girlfriends of the children and grandchildren, and important family friends, such as godparents, honorary aunts and uncles, and so forth.

But some of the elders' families do not look like this at all. For example, one elder we spoke with said, "I raised myself. I was ten years old when I started working, because my parents died. At the age of fourteen, I had my first child. I raised all my children, working very hard to raise them."

Another elder, a man who had no wife or children, had lived in the United States more than seventy years. His blood relatives were all still in Central America, but he explained that he "built" his family here from friends, coworkers, and their families.

One man's children had all moved to distant cities, but he kept his sense of family through daily calls with them and through attending a senior center where, he said with a sweep of his hand, "We are all family here."

Many of our Latino elders are original immigrants from elsewhere in the New World. If *their* families are so different, our younger generation families must be even more varied. Indeed, as we dig deeper and deeper into the idea of family, we find that no matter what we think a family should look like, there are many kinds of families.

Shared activities, attributes, and obligations help make a family *feel* like a family. We can say that families have qualities of love, connections, friendship, loyalty, obligation, joy, mutual care, and even legal expectations. But these qualities of family are displayed and reinforced in many ways:

- being together for celebrations, especially important milestones, such as baptisms, birthdays, graduations, *quinciñeras*, weddings, and funerals
- sharing mutual obligations, such as looking after each other's children, setting good examples for younger members of the family, or contributing money, food, or time to family needs
- sharing meals
- communicating with each other in person, on the phone, via email, letters, or by other means

All human beings, no matter where they are from, have an instinctive need to feel a *sense of connection with others,* also called a *sense of belonging.* We want to be needed by others and we want to serve others. We want to belong to a group. We gain a sense of identity, a sense of self-worth, a sense of significance through our connections.

Our connections help us deal with our own personal struggles. Just as important, our connections help us to help *others face their* challenges. When we help a family member, we feel needed and worthy. When family members help us, they feel needed and worthy. This exchange creates a happy circle of belonging that helps us feel secure. For most of us, this sense of belonging extends to other circles that include our community, our congregation, members of associations we participate in, and our workmates.

### Many family assets

Many Latinos have large families. Most of us enjoy having many people around us. Most of us have an inclusive sense of family that embraces many people beyond blood relatives.

We love to celebrate, too, and celebrations always include food. Our meals give us a chance to talk and remember the places and people we left behind.

It is no wonder that our wise elders would claim family as an important cultural asset. The large family is really one of our great strengths. Our course, in a marriage, our spouse and our children are the very first priority, but everyone else is very close behind. The large extended family helps in many ways:

- We help each other find jobs.
- We save money by sharing child-care duties.
- We model our values for each other and help keep each other "in line."
- We share expenses.
- When there is a family celebration, everyone brings something. Even if we have no job and little money, we find something to bring.

It is in our families that we learn the value of belonging, as well as practices such as *respeto* and *personalismo.* Research into Latino families has shown that Latinos who immigrate continue to strongly value close family life even as they become more and more accustomed to the U.S. culture.[6] But this research also shows that as the next generations grow up here, they likely place less value on a close extended family.

Our strong family connections are very important as we build lives in our new home. Research has shown that our extended family networks, family cohesion, and high levels of social support form a "protective factor." That means that our extended family connections help protect against negative consequences of poverty and other challenges, such as early sexual behavior, and tobacco, alcohol, or drug use.

Inez, a middle-aged mother of seven, tells this story:

> ▪ ▪ ▪ *I was talking with my friend, a white woman whose family had been in the U.S. for centuries—since before it declared independence from England. We are very close and were comparing family notes. I was telling her about the time I had to confront my sister's daughter, who had been using drugs and who looked like she was getting involved in some risky sex too. My friend was amazed that I'd even talk about that or that I'd be okay confronting my niece. She said the same problems happened in her family, but those things were private or kept a secret, or at least they weren't talked about except between parent and child. And her sister-in-law would have been very angry if my friend had "butted in" to a private family matter.* ▪ ▪ ▪

In our families, parents take primary responsibility for children, but they share that with other family members, such as aunts, uncles, and grandparents. In most of our families, these helpers are welcome to come to the parents and say, "I see your child may be in trouble." Our willingness to share the responsibility for raising children is a great asset. Our children's value of *respeto* also means they are likely to listen to the wise counsel of someone older.

It is interesting to observe how the concept of "family" differs from one culture to another. For example, it is normal for a Latino client to visit a counselor with much of his or her family alongside. But in more mainstream families, only the client comes. Whatever personal problem has caused the person to visit a counselor is more private. In many Latino families, the weight of a problem can be spread among others to lighten its load.

Even routine tasks are often shared, as Sebastian pointed out. He recently had to move from his studio apartment to a larger place in the same building. "I could have moved everything myself in about three hours," he said. "But on moving day, there were my cousins and brothers and uncles, and we had me moved in twenty minutes.

Meanwhile, my sister and aunts cleaned the old apartment. Within an hour, my new place was all set up, and we sat down to eat. And I never had to ask anyone for help. They just all knew I was moving and they showed up."

Just as Sebastian's family made his workload easy, the family can share the burden of problems and troubles. That mutual support is a keystone of our loving families.

Our cultural values and immigration experiences also translate into strong family relationships and good parenting practices that help protect our young people against many problems. For example:

- Latino parents show a great ability to adapt their parenting strategies to the new culture: Latino teens whose parents use effective parenting practices and monitor their children are less likely to be sexually active.[7]

- Our value of respecting older people makes it a duty for the older siblings to set a good example for the younger. When *respeto* is working well in a family, younger children look and learn from the examples set by the older children.

- Our experience in immigrating has shown us just how very tough we are. We can call on this same strength to overcome other troubles—as well as to claim new opportunities.

### Dating, marriage, and intercultural families

Among more traditional Latinos and those who have recently immigrated, people often seek to meet and marry someone who is from the same region or country. This arises out of a wish to preserve traditions and to feel comfortable. Ignacio, a social worker, was born in the United States, but his parents and extended family had come from El Salvador. He described his experience this way.

> ■ ■ ■ *I was beginning to date, and my family, especially my aunts, kept asking about who I was going out with and where she was from. I was dating classmates, and they were from all parts of the world. My family members kept asking questions. I looked around at my aunts and thought, "How is it that all the way up here in Milwaukee, they managed to find guys from El Salvador to marry? Obviously, that didn't happen by chance." I knew that if I found a girlfriend who was at least from the same country, things would go easier for me and for her, but everyone I meet is from all over the place, and that's interesting to me. I felt some pressure from my family, but I knew*

*that what really concerned them was "Would she like the foods we like, the dances and music we like, the soccer team we like?" It was about them feeling comfortable with someone who might become part of the family.* ■■■

Although most of us won't talk about it openly, race and class are issues that enter into decisions about whom we date. Prejudice is something many Latinos face, but it is also something we carry with us. In many of our countries of origin, the disparity between rich and poor is enormous. There are few opportunities to move up in the world. But here, the boundaries between classes are more fluid. Intercultural and interracial marriages are increasingly common.

Although many first-generation Latinos marry someone from their country or region of origin, their children, who have been raised in the United States, often marry outside their ethnic origins. This should not be a surprise; we settle in and raise our children in diverse neighborhoods. Nevertheless, intercultural families can surprise some first-generation parents and may require some adjustments.

Intercultural couples may face pressure from their families, and on first introduction of an outsider, the family members can be tough on him or her, as well as on their family member. But at the end of the day, rarely is anyone rejected. We hear things like, "Okay, he's African American, and we're not used to that, but he loves Tia Carlotta's tamales." At a certain point, we *are* family.

### Parenting skills

Our lives may be blessed by young children, but they are also a challenge. They learn English quickly, and we may have to rely on them to be interpreters. This shifts the power in the family! We are accustomed to expecting our children to respect us, but when our children are translating what teachers or other authorities say, they can bend the truth. The children can feel isolated too. They may feel trapped between the culture of their parents and the culture of the other kids around them. When the family is out of balance like this, the children can be at greater risk of getting involved in troubles, such as using tobacco, alcohol, or drugs, joining gang activity, or having early sex. Teens earnestly seek some way to fit in, and unfortunately, these troubling activities offer a quick set of peers to hang out with.

For this reason, it is especially important that Latino parents develop good parenting skills. Let's start by understanding the normal developmental steps of children from infancy to maturity.

### Stages of development

Psychologists have studied children from all over the world. We now know there are certain stages that most healthy children and adolescents go through as they mature, regardless of where they are born. It helps for everyone in the family to understand these stages, since grandparents, aunts and uncles, and cousins may all be involved in raising our children.

Sometimes parents grow frustrated when a child doesn't do the things that the parent expects. Yet this may be because the child is simply unable to, or unable to understand what the parent wants. Therefore, understanding these stages can help parents develop realistic expectations of their child. At the same time, sometimes children are far behind the normal developmental stages. If we know these stages and see that our child is lagging behind, we can talk to a doctor to see whether the child needs assistance.

### Infancy (birth to twelve months)[8]

The early infant has very little control over her body, but rapidly develops new skills. Here are some important milestones she will likely experience:

- rolling over at four to six months
- sitting up unassisted by six months
- babbling and squealing between four and six months

---

**Free parenting book**

The U.S. National Institutes of Health has a free parenting book for you. *¿Qué Significa ser Padres?* was written in 2006 and offers parenting strategies based on scientific research. You can view it online at www.nichd.nih.gov/publications/pubs/documents /que_significa_ser_padres_espanol.pdf or order a copy by calling 1-800-370-2943 (8:30 a.m. – 4 p.m. eastern standard time). The book is available in English as well, under the title *Adventures in Parenting*.

---

- crawling, possibly walking, by twelve months
- picking up and putting down small objects, by twelve months
- possibly speaking simple words, such as "mama," "papa," or "no," by twelve months
- feeling shy or anxious with strangers, possibly crying when mother or father leaves
- possibly testing parental responses during feedings or in response to her behavior, for example, trying to see what you will do if she refuses food or if she cries after you leave the room

### Toddlers (age one to two years)[9]

The child at this age quickly becomes more independent. At this age the child has very little self-control. He doesn't understand how to play with others, but he will play alongside them. However, it is not uncommon for the toddler to hit, yell, and become upset when trying to share a toy with another child. He may have tantrums, and sometimes parents call this age the "terrible twos" because of the demands and tantrums. Here are some of the behaviors you will observe:

- walking and running
- kicking a ball
- walking up and down stairs with help
- carrying objects
- scribbling
- building block towers
- beginning to feed himself
- understanding and speaking 500 to 700 words
- using simple phrases and two- to four-word sentences
- following simple instructions
- imitating adults and other children
- becoming more independent, possibly showing defiant behavior

*Preschool (ages three to five years)*[10]

During these years, the child's world is filled with fantasy and imagination. She may not understand the difference between her fantasies and the real world. She can be heard inventing stories while playing with toys or when talking to family. She becomes interested in new experiences and learns to cooperate with other children. She can dress and undress herself. She can follow simple commands and recall parts of a story. As she becomes four years and older, she can become bossy, very energetic, and she may misbehave and challenge parents in ways that remind them of when she was two. All of the imagination and "testing" help the child build a secure foundation in readiness for kindergarten. She will make true friends, share, take turns, and show empathy toward others. Here are some activities the child begins doing during this time:

- standing on one foot, hopping, swinging, climbing, doing somersaults
- throwing a ball overhand and maybe catching a bounced ball
- copying shapes; drawing circles, triangles, and squares; maybe drawing letters
- dressing and undressing
- usually taking care of own toilet needs
- counting to ten or more, using sentences, naming at least four colors
- wanting to please friends and to be like her friends
- negotiating solutions to conflicts
- sometimes being demanding, sometimes eager to cooperate

*Grade school children (six to twelve years)*[11]

During this span, the child becomes increasingly independent. At the younger ages of this stage, children are more reliant on their parents for their emotional and social needs, but as the children grow, their peers become more and more important. Their motor skills improve, and they may become involved in sports, music, dance, and other cultural pursuits. Their weight and height increase at steady rates. Emotionally and physically, the child will show this developmental growth:

- increasing ability to interact with peers
- having more same-sex friends
- engaging in competitive activities
- developing and testing values and beliefs

- identifying with a group, defining self through peers
- seeking to gain a sense of mastery based on physical and emotional control and school performance
- thinking logically
- gaining an improved sense of time
- copying adult speech patterns

### Early adolescence (ten to twelve years old)

- possibly beginning puberty
- changing body proportions become similar to those of an adult
- succeeding in school becomes increasingly important
- increasing ability to think abstractly
- despite abstract thinking skills, not making many intellectual leaps, possibly not reasoning hypothetically or inferring motives
- answering "who," "what," "where," and "when" questions but possibly still having problems answering "why"

### Middle adolescence (thirteen to seventeen years)[12]

By the end of this time, most children have reached 95 percent of their eventual adult height. They are concerned about their personal attractiveness. They can be very energetic one moment and lethargic the next. Secondary sexual characteristics have developed. Romantic attachments may begin, and sexual experimentation is not uncommon. Intellectually, they have increasing powers of abstract thought, but they will revert back to using concrete thought under stress. They have a better understanding of cause-and-effect relationships. The adolescent can show quick mood swings, and his emotional changes during this time can be stressful for families:

- possibly developing conflicts with family as the adolescent seeks independence
- identifying with peers, wanting to fit in and follow fads
- beginning to experiment with adult roles and behaviors, including sex, drugs, alcohol, tobacco, and risk-taking, accompanied by the thought that negative consequences "can't happen to me"

- likely working at his first job
- testing new values and ideas, and maybe (temporarily) rejecting parental values and ideas
- struggling to develop a sense of personal identity

### The basic skills of a parent

Understanding these important developmental stages is a start. But guiding your child through them while maintaining your own peace of mind can be quite a challenge! Above all, parents need to interact with their children frequently, show them love, play with them, and help them reach important milestones. These are skills we parents should hold ourselves accountable for:

1. *Have appropriate expectations of our child.*

   - Understand child growth and development and what can be expected when (as we just described). For example, it is not realistic to expect a toddler to understand the simple instructions that a five-year-old would.

   - Allow children to exhibit normal developmental behaviors. For example, older infants may cry when parents leave, toddlers may have temper tantrums, preschoolers will tell stories that are based on fantasy rather than truth, grade-schoolers will want to spend time playing with their peers, and so forth.

   - See yourself as a caregiver. As parents, we are responsible for taking care of our children or seeing that they are taken care of by another responsible person who understands appropriate expectations for our children.

2. *Have empathy for our child.*

   - We must understand and value a child's needs even if those needs seem silly to us. For example, a preschooler or grade-schooler may be afraid of the dark or envision monsters that are not there. We need to put ourselves in the child's shoes as we comfort and explain that there are no monsters.

   - Recognize the complex feelings of children. Just as we have complicated feelings, so do children. They need us to show that we understand and respect their feelings, even when those feelings are contrary to our expectations. For example, a child may be angry if we ask him to take out the garbage. We can acknowledge that he is angry even when we continue to demand that he play his role in the family by taking the garbage out.

- Understand the importance of encouraging a child's positive growth. Our job as parents is not only to feed and clothe our children. It is just as important that we help them move in a positive direction. We can explain positive values to them and we can praise their positive behavior, or explain what was wrong with negative behavior.

- Understand the importance of communicating with our child. Children need communication—they need to know that we love and care for them, that we are interested in what they are thinking and doing. And they need to know what we are thinking about.

3. *Use appropriate, positive discipline.*

- Understand and use alternatives to physical punishment. Some of our parents may have used spanking, hitting, slapping, and other physical punishments, but we know today that there are better ways to steer our children in the right direction. Rewarding desirable behavior is more effective than punishing unwanted behavior. Physical punishment may harm the child physically and psychologically, and parents may encounter legal difficulties as a result (see *Responding to your child's behavior*).

- Understand the importance of including all the family members in establishing family rules and accepting that the rules are for the whole family, not just the child. A few clear rules are better than lots of rules. And the child can't know the rules if we don't explain them.

- Value a mutual parent-child relationship. One way of expressing our sense of *familismo* is to take time to see our children as the individuals they are, get to know them, and help them get to know us. This relationship also makes it easier when we need to correct a child's behavior.

- Respect children and their needs.

**4.** *Understand appropriate family roles.*

- Parents need to find comfort, support, and companionship from adult friends, not from their children. Sometimes when one parent leaves, is not in the country yet, or is emotionally unavailable, the sole partner can lean on a child for companionship. This disrupts the natural role of the parent as a guide and the child as a learner and, as a result, can harm the child's emotional development.

- Understand the importance of being responsible for your own behavior. Children do not "make" us do things. We react or we respond to them, and we need to hold ourselves accountable by valuing our parenting successes and learning from—and correcting—our parenting mistakes.

- Understand the value of a caregiver feeling worthy as a person. Our children need love and respect from us to feel worthy. It is very difficult to give what we ourselves lack. Therefore, we need to take care of ourselves and our needs to be sure that we can be good caregivers for our children.

- Understand that children should be allowed to express themselves. Some people have said that "children are to be seen and not heard," but this is incorrect. Children need to express themselves. We need to teach them ways to respectfully express their thoughts and feelings.

**5.** *Help children gain power and independence.*

- Our job as parents is to help our children grow into respectable, independent adults who contribute to the world. We can do this by helping our children learn to make good choices, letting them make mistakes that will not harm them, and helping them learn to deal with the consequences of their choices.

- Understand the value of encouraging children to express their views while still cooperating with us. Our children can learn to respectfully tell us what they think while still following the family rules and expectations. This helps them prepare to be independent adults in society, where they will often face similar circumstances.

- Value our children's ability to solve problems. When our children are on their own, they will need to be able to solve problems without us. Children have remarkable skills. As they age, we will see their increased capacity to solve problems. Sometimes we want to step in and rescue them from their mistakes, but they can learn by figuring out how to resolve some of the challenges they face on their own. This does not mean that we abandon them to solve all their problems alone. Our job is to support them as they learn to solve problems.

### Family communication

Keeping family communication going when we are working so much and the children are busy with school projects can be difficult. But good communication is vital. When a young couple learns to communicate well with each other, later when they have children, their children will learn by example.

Good communication means that we express ourselves appropriately, that we are heard, and that we listen. Listening can't happen when people raise their voices—after all, if two people are yelling at each other, *no one is listening*. Communication is a two-way process. We need to really hear and understand what someone says to us, and vice versa.

Many things can get in the way of good communication:

- We assume we know what other people think. For example, just as Andrea is about to explain why she can't look after her younger brother, her mother says, "I know, you want to go out with your girlfriends." Imagine how Andrea would feel if her real reason was that she needed those two hours to complete a big assignment for history class.

- We assume that other people *should* know what we think. For example, Marta is angry because she prepared a special meal for Nestor, who came home late. He didn't know she was making a special meal, and Marta didn't know that Nestor was late because he was shopping for a present for her.

- We assume that we know what is right for someone and try to convince them without listening. For example, Benjamin is excited about his new job as an assistant at the library, but his father insists he work as a carpenter—ignoring the fact that Benjamin is not good with tools but is very skilled with words.

- We bring up issues unrelated to what's going on. For example, Jesse is trying to explain why he thinks the family needs to trim its budget and Elena brings up the time he stayed out late at a bar.

We can do many things to improve communication. Just like any skill, good communication takes a method, and it takes practice. One of the most important methods is called "active listening."

### Active listening

Active listening is a way of letting other people know that we are paying attention and trying to understand them. Active listening helps us avoid the assumptions that we just described. Listening actively is useful all the time, but especially when there is stress or disagreement. Start by making sure there are no distractions, such as television, radio, video games, cooking, or cleaning. When we use active listening, we need to focus on the task, which is understanding the person or people communicating with us. We listen carefully and really try to understand what the people are saying. When they have finished, we try to say back to them what we just heard, exactly word for word.

So Nestor might say, "I hear that you are angry because I came home late. It sounds like you wanted to surprise me with a special meal. I can understand that you are upset." When Marta hears that Nestor understands, she is ready to hear what he has to say. By using active listening, they can turn a situation that might have been damaging to their relationship into one in which they both realize they had been trying to make each other happy with a special surprise.

Of course, in a larger family, things get much more complicated. Imagine five people trying to be understood and to understand each other! In a family, we have to balance the needs and wants of many different people. No wonder we have conflicts! It's not possible for everyone to get what they want or need at the time they want it. Sometimes the parents must step in with priorities about budget, the needs of younger children, their own job requirements, and so forth. But even then, children can be involved in a way that helps them understand the decision.

*Family meetings*

One way to work toward balancing multiple needs is to hold family meetings. During these meetings, everyone gets time to speak about what they need, and no one can talk while someone else is talking. Everyone needs to use the active listening skills we've described—to the degree they are able. (Young children obviously can't do this.) And everyone can chip in with solutions that might help the situation. You can even make a list and then work together to choose the ideas that seem to have the best chance of working. When the children are involved in solving problems, they will be more enthusiastic about participating in the solutions—even when those solutions call for some extra work or sacrifice for them.

## Maintaining discipline at home

The elders we consulted advised that *respeto* is important, but they also said that respect is a two-way street. Anita, an elder who lives in a house with her daughter, son-in-law, and grandchildren, said this:

> ■■■ *If we want to receive respect from our children, we have to give respect to them, too, and be an example. If parents don't teach respect, children take their own path. And if the parents don't step in and get them on the right path, the family can start to fall apart. If there is no communication about this in the family, children will start to do whatever they want.* ■■■

We have a saying, "Teach your children to respect you, not to fear you." Psychologists tell us there are many ways to maintain discipline that do not involve physical or emotional punishment. These methods work better than physical punishment. Physical punishment can injure the child and cause the child to associate negative feelings with the person who punishes them. Even though some of us were raised by parents who considered physical punishment acceptable, today we advise a better method. As parents, we need to learn this method, and we also need to be sure that everyone who helps care for our children follows our lead.

There are three parts to positive discipline:

- We establish a home that encourages appropriate behavior.

- We respond appropriately and consistently to our child's behavior.
- And then we observe and resolve difficult behavior.

### *Establish a home that encourages appropriate behavior*

We can easily fall into the habit of reacting only whenever our child misbehaves. However, it is better to plan for good behavior and *immediately* reward our child for doing something positive—or at least trying to. So if we find our young daughter trying to share with her little brother, immediately praise her for what she did right.

Make it easy to succeed by making your directions simple, direct, and clear. Even as adults, we have an easier time understanding simple directions than complicated ones. Think how much harder this is for our children! For example, don't say, "The doll should not be left on the floor." Instead say, "Pick up the doll. Then put it on the shelf." Have only a few rules and repeat them often. Let the child know immediately when a rule has been broken. Only add new rules gradually.

Get a plan ready for times that you know will be difficult. This means we must observe our child and remember when he is most likely to misbehave. If our child begs for a toy or candy every time we take him to the store, then we can reduce the problem by thinking ahead. We can develop a plan with the child to reward him for not begging. We can find someone to watch him while we run to the store. Or we can plan our route through the store to avoid the things our child begs for.

### *Respond appropriately and consistently*

Rewarding good behavior is much more effective than punishing bad behavior. Rewards help our children feel good about themselves. Sometimes punishment is useful, so long as it does not physically harm or abuse, humiliate, or otherwise emotionally harm the child. Punishment only works if it is consistent and immediately follows the misbehavior. If we have to punish our child often, it may be a sign that we have too many rules or that the rules are not appropriate for our child's stage of development. Frequent punishment can result in a child who feels that she is a bad person, and she may continue to misbehave because punishment seems unavoidable.

Punishments work best when they are natural consequences of the misbehavior. For example, if the child was supposed to put his toys away and did not, the consequence may be that he does not get to play with the toys for the rest of the day. This links his decision not to put toys away with his privilege of playing with toys. Sometimes the natural consequence can be bad for our child or someone else. Instead, we can use penalties, such as removing a privilege (no television for the day) or a "time-out," which is quiet time away from others. A good guideline is one minute of time-out per year of age. For example, a five-year-old gets five minutes of time-out as a penalty.

Ignoring misbehavior that is annoying but not harmful can gradually eliminate the unwanted behavior. As long as the misbehavior is not going to hurt the child or someone else, we can avoid responding to it and instead provide praise for good behavior. For example, we can ignore whining and begging, instead praising our child when she asks directly for what she wants.

### *Observe and resolve difficult behavior*

Sometimes our children misbehave again and again in ways that are very frustrating. The first step is to try to find out what benefit the child is seeking from the behavior. What usually happens after the misbehavior? That can help us understand why the child is misbehaving. Then we need to develop consequences—rewards and punishments—that particularly matter to our child. If our child really loves a certain show, we can punish them by withdrawing that show or reward them by granting extra time to watch the show.

Sometimes children's misbehavior can be a sign of some other issue affecting the child. When misbehavior persists and you cannot resolve it using positive methods such as those we've described, seek help. Many parents find that an outside perspective from a counselor can help them resolve difficult situations.[13]

### Helping children do well in school[14]

When we asked their advice for younger generations reading this book, the circle of elders with whom we spoke said, "Study, get an education, and be prepared for a good job. At the end of the day you are only worth what you know."

But helping our children do well in school can be very difficult when we work two jobs, come home late, and have to manage so many tasks. Some of us have limited English skills and are unaccustomed to the U.S. educational system and its expectations.

Despite these challenges, we can do a lot to help our children do well. One of the first things we can do is to be sure that they know we care about their school success. We need to repeat this message often and we must follow through on it. We must be sure our children are registered for school, attend daily, and do their homework. We must meet with our children's teachers, and we must check our children's work and progress. When they are struggling, we can help by supporting them emotionally and by helping them reach out to their teachers for additional instruction and advice. And we can show our pride when they work hard, rewarding them with praise for their efforts and successes.

Children value our praise and our opinions, which is why we must instill the value of education from an early age. Some parents have found that setting clear expectations helps:

- attending school daily
- completing homework immediately after school
- discussing academic challenges with us so we can guide them to the help they need
- high school graduation followed by enrollment in post-secondary training, such as community college, college, or vocational-technical school

Along with these expectations, we also need to practice encouraging behaviors, such as:

- providing children with a quiet place to study and ensuring that younger children do not bother older ones who are studying
- discussing schoolwork and new knowledge at the family meal
- setting an example of reading books daily
- celebrating achievements, whether small or big
- helping children divide complex goals and assignments into small, manageable ones (for example, writing one page of a fifteen-page term paper each day rather than writing it all in one night)
- starting with first grade, setting a practice of monitoring school work, attendance, and participation in school activities
- taking advantage of minority advancement programs (for example, programs that encourage the first generation to go to college)

One of our Latino elders shared her experience with education: "I raised my grand-child from when he was just born. I would take him to school and pick him up. I encouraged him to learn, because I did not have that opportunity. He continued to study and learn, and today he is very thankful to me for teaching him the importance of education. He is now the president of the local community center."

### Our elders

Elders are very important. Understanding the attitudes of our elders helps the outsider gain a better understanding of *familismo*. In many of our home countries, the household often includes grandparents, parents, and grandchildren. In some of our home countries this is less typical. For non-Latinos in the United States, the elders do not usually live with their children and may even live far from them. We are accustomed to caring for our elders to their final days.

Regardless of which Latin American country we originate from, most of us believe that elders are due respect. But the ways we show that respect may have to change in our new home. In the United States, work schedules and housing availability diminish the kind of closeness we were accustomed to. This can be hard for elders *and* for children and grandchildren: the elder expects a certain kind of treatment, while the more acculturated younger children do not feel obligated to provide that level of attention.

Some families work hard to help elders assimilate, but their elders resist that help. These conflicts may be out in the open, or hidden. For example, Consuelo, now in her fifties, immigrated with her mother, father, and siblings when she was a young girl. She is very acculturated. Her father has now passed away, and her mother lives with her. She has many friends of similar age and background:

■■■ *I see some of my friends will speak to their parents only in English. The parents may answer back in Spanish, but the children insist on speaking English to their parents. It is different in our family. My mother would get very angry if I did that. I speak to her in Spanish out of respect. When I talk to my friends about this, though, their belief is that their parents need to learn English. I can see both sides of the issue. You do want your parents to be able to communicate in English, but you also want to show your respect.* ■■■

Life in the United States can be isolating for our elders, especially if they arrive after we do. Sometimes they rely completely on us and our children. They don't reach out and establish a network of their own. Yet the families of younger generations are often much smaller than they would have been in the home country. That means that the elders have a smaller network of support. Here, where everyone is expected to be very independent regardless of age, this can be a trial.

"I talk to my mother every day, and I talk to my father, who lives in Texas, every week," explained Irene. "They'd be furious if I didn't call them. It's my responsibility. But my husband is African American. He can't believe how much I talk to my family. But I'm just as surprised that he only calls his parents once a month. That seems to be enough for them, but I need to know how everyone is all the time, and they want to know about me just as much." Irene can drop in on any member of her family whenever she wants, and it's no surprise. But her husband's family expects an invitation or a call first.

Most of us continue to consult our elders on family matters, and they expect us to. They provide guidance on raising a family, making job decisions, moving, and everything important. This is a duty for life. They feel the need to continue to guide their adult children, and they feel very responsible for helping to raise their grandkids. One often sees elders in mainstream culture moving to a warmer climate, away from kids and grandkids; however, it is very rare for a Latino grandparent to say, "My work is done; those are *their* kids. I'll watch them from time to time, but raising them—well, that's their problem."

We have heard the saying "It takes a village to raise a child," but for many Latino elders, this saying is a way of life. Elders are comfortable correcting the behavior of those younger than them. Their sense of family is broader and more inclusive than that of the mainstream culture.

### Wisdom from our elders

Regarding *familismo,* our group of elders offered this advice for younger generations, as well as those who are recently arriving in the United States:

- The biggest challenges are keeping the culture alive within the family and retaining values from our home culture. It is important to learn both languages and cultures, but be sure to keep your culture and roots alive within the family.

- We want to be respected, but if we want respect, we have to give respect to our children and teach them what respect looks like. We can't ask them to give something that we're not willing to give ourselves. If parents don't teach respect, children take their own path, and that can tear the family apart.

- Children need love. Do not mistreat them or use bad language. Give yourself completely to the care of your children. You must be a good example to them so that they can learn to show love when they have a family.

- Be happy with other people and accept them as they are. Treat each other well, and treat everyone around you well, because we are all united. For example, if someone gossips about you and you hear about it, don't worry; just show the gossiper even more love and respect than before.

- To keep the family together, communicate often. Check in with each other, hang out together, talk a lot, got to parks, share meals, and celebrate together. Constant communication keeps families going.

- If the parents have some sort of a problem or are having a discussion or an argument, they should discuss it among themselves and not involve their children. This is showing respect to the children, who can't be expected to understand. If you teach your children this, then as they get older, they will teach their own children—they will model it for their own children.

- One has to be a parent, a friend, and a confidant. Children must trust us. For example, if they are having a problem with a friend or coworker, it is good for the parent to know about the problem, so the child can ask for help and the parent can give guidance.

- Encourage grandchildren to study and learn and prepare for a good job. Always wish the best for them.

- This is a good place to raise families. Just be very careful about the people your children hang out with. You must be watchful to be sure that your children follow your expectations.

- Be hard working, and be good citizens of the community.

- Take care of your parents, respect them, and love them and their families.

*Caring for our elders*

Elders offer wise guidance, consolation, a connection to our cultural origins, a sense of belonging, and a secure feeling of our place in the future (giving us the sense that "one day this will be my role"). They also offer practical help—for example, caring for grandchildren. But elders have needs too. In some cases, the practices they learned growing up should be replaced by better practices.

Here are just a few of our elders' needs:

- good health care
- a better understanding of the importance of good nutrition and physical fitness for maintaining a good quality of life
- a basic understanding of how to navigate the new culture's health services, social services, and financial systems

Diet and nutrition can be especially challenging. Obesity and adult-onset diabetes are major illnesses among Latinos. Both are thought to be linked to a lower quality of physical fitness and nutrition. It can be difficult to educate an elder about changes that contribute to better health. First, the value of *respeto* suggests that we not tell elders what to do. Even when we have their best interests at heart, elders may perceive our attempts to improve their diet as challenging their authority, not to mention trying to remove something they really enjoy.

Fortunately, some elders respond to the message "I love you and need you around, and the grandchildren need you too. We want you to have a long and healthy life. We are not trying to tell you what to do, but we have learned new things about what causes illness and what contributes to good health. We want you to make some small changes to your diet and activity to be sure that you are here with us for a long time."

Sometimes elders who do not want to change their eating and activity habits may respond better to the same advice when it comes from a professional nutritionist or physician as well as from their beloved family.

Some illnesses are *acute*. This means the person becomes ill, and then recovers (or tragically, passes away) in a relatively short time—a few weeks or months. Other diseases are *chronic*. This means the person lives with the disease for many months or years. Often there is no cure. Alzheimer's disease, dementia, diabetes, Parkinson's disease, and other chronic illnesses that aging people acquire require special care.

Most of us want to keep our aging relatives with us, at home, or else very nearby. Caring for a person with a chronic disease is challenging and exhausting. The person we take care of may be a spouse, a parent, or another relative. We would like to think that love can solve all problems, but the reality is that we need help with this. In the process of caring for our elder, we often forget to take care of ourselves. This is bad for us and it is bad for our loved one, because if we don't take care of ourselves, we will lack the energy to take care of our loved one. Then we get angry with ourselves because we feel we are failing at our duty and goal to care for the people we love. As an example, here's Luciano's story.

Luciano's mother was diagnosed with Alzheimer's disease when she was in her late seventies. For the first few years, Luciano was able to help his mother quite a bit. He helped with medical care, he kept her active, he kept her in touch with her friends, and he helped her remember things. But as her disease progressed, things got more difficult for Luciano. His own wife had passed away and his children had moved out and started their own families. His mother's illness required that he spend more and more time with her just to be sure she did not harm herself or wander off. He took early retirement so he could be home to care for her, as he thought a good son should. But even that did not seem to be enough. At times he felt so sad he would shut his windows and weep in private. His lovely mother was no longer the same person. Sometimes she called him by her father's name, by her brothers' names, or worst of all, by his own father's name. He felt confused and tired. He felt as though he was failing her.

He did not know what do to. His children were so busy with the grandchildren, and he did not want to bother them for help. They seemed not to notice the difference in their grandmother's behavior, or would ignore the problem. But his friends noticed how rarely he went out. And one of them told him she took her mother to a nearby senior center twice a week. When Luciano called the center, he learned that it offered a class about caregiving for a loved one who has Alzheimer's. He also got the phone number for the local chapter of the Alzheimer's Association, which had many resources for him. In class, he was able to share his worry, guilt, and frustration with other people in the same situation. He found out about other social services that could share some of his burden. And he developed a plan to seek help, reach out to his children for help, and reconnect with friends, so he could keep his mental and physical energy up and continue to help his mother.

As Luciano did, we need to learn to take care of ourselves even as we take care of our elders. This means we must keep these things in mind:

- *Understand that we are not alone.* Other people face these very same issues, and we can find help by talking to them and to social service agencies.

- *Take responsibility for our own physical and emotional health.* We can't give our loved one good care if we sacrifice so much that we fail to meet our own needs.

- *Have realistic expectations about what we can and can't do to help our loved one.* We need to educate ourselves about the nature of our loved one's illness, what can be expected, and just how much we can do to help.

- *Focus on the things we can do to help.* When we help a person who has a chronic illness, we may feel as though we are trying to hold back the ocean tide. To stay well, we must celebrate the things we have done to help, let go of those things that we cannot change, and seek assistance when we can.

- *Tell other people what we need.* People can't help us unless we reach out, explain our troubles, and accept the assistance they have to offer. Luciano was finally able to tell his children about the problem, as well as some close friends. Soon they were bringing him meals, offering to watch his mother, and giving him breaks so he could restore his energy and health.

- *Manage our emotions.* Just as the waves of the sea pulse up and down, our happiness, sadness, excitement, and weariness come in waves. We can learn to manage these emotions so that we stay in control, just as an expert seaman navigates the waves.

- *Set realistic goals for ourselves and our loved one.* For example, Luciano still had a house to manage, with projects like painting and repair work. He found ways to break these jobs into small tasks that he could do while his mother slept. Once, he would have painted an entire room at one time, but now he painted just a doorway while his mother napped, and then a wall the next day, and another wall the next, until the job was done.

**Tips for caregivers**

Many of us follow the tradition of living near to our elders or of having them live with us. As our parents and grandparents age, their needs increase, especially if they experience health problems. To be good caregivers, we need to take care of ourselves too. The following tips will help us:

- Educate yourself about the needs of your beloved elder.
- Ask for help from other people.
- Be willing to accept help.
- Don't isolate yourself, and don't wrap yourself up in the problem.
- Use community resources to get the help you need.

The U.S. government runs a free service to help people find care for elders. The Eldercare Locator offers many resources. Call the service at **1-800-677-1116** (both Spanish and English speakers will be available) or visit the website at www.eldercare.gov.

## The impact of immigration and acculturation on the family

Immigration and acculturation offer many opportunities, but also create stresses in the family. In this section, we will look at how immigration and acculturation change gender roles, create conflict between generations, and stress relationships. (The personal experience of being an immigrant is addressed in chapter 6.)

### Changing gender roles

Kiko, a social worker and relationship counselor, says that at least some of the struggles he sees in Latino marriages grow from traditional gender roles that do not work in the U.S. economy. Traditional Latino families expect that men should be the primary breadwinners and women should manage the households. But in the United States, women may find work more easily than men do. Many of the available jobs are in fields where, traditionally, we would not expect men to work. The impossibility of fulfilling these gender expectations can create conflict in a family. Here's how Kiko put it:

■ ■ ■ *There are some things about our culture that we need to leave behind, like the sexism and inequality in genders. These expectations can really thwart a happy relationship. If a man is not expected to cook, but needs to or wants to, it becomes a pressure issue for both the man and the woman in a relationship. If both of you have worked, why should the man get to relax while the woman cooks and cleans? I have even seen relationships where the man can't find work and the woman works all day, comes home, and still she's supposed to buy the groceries, cook, clean, do the dishes, and then do the laundry while the man continues to relax.*

*These expectations no longer work in most households in the United States. The expectations create a lot of tension in the marriage. And the pressures may come from outside. For example, the man and woman may both feel that if he cooked and cleaned, he'd be less of a man. Yet there she is, exhausted, and she can't bring herself to the relationship, and meanwhile, he feels useless. It's a recipe for misery, because the ingredients—gender expectations—are spoiled!*

*The transition can be hard, and the pressures are not just limited to the people in the relationship. For example, I know young couples where the husband and wife are both comfortable with doing jobs they traditionally aren't expected to do. But the wife will say, "Don't tell your mom that I don't always iron your shirts." Meanwhile, her husband says, "I feel terrible that she even worries about this. I can iron my own shirts, and she's just as busy as I am. I'm happy to iron her clothes when she needs it too." They are happy—it is the social expectations about gender roles that bother them.*

*It's really a shame. Guys are worried about what other people will think if they cook, and women are worried about what other people will think if they hate to cook. What's the point in that? But breaking these roles is stressful.* ■ ■ ■

In many cases, the gender roles that are strong in traditional Latino culture are not conducive to individual or family happiness. The transition can be difficult. It helps to explore the ways in which these expectations, or rules, put unfair burdens on each other. For each of these rules, we need to think about these questions:

- Where did we learn this rule?
- Who "wrote" this rule?
- Who benefits from the rule?

- Does the rule make sense in the place we live now and in the economic conditions we face?
- Is this rule fair?

### Conflict between generations

Once we are in the new culture, change is inevitable. Some of us work very hard to preserve our cultural traditions, language, and values, and we may live in neighborhoods populated largely by people from regions near where we grew up. Others of us live in very diverse neighborhoods or in largely mainstream neighborhoods. Some of us actively seek to adopt the new customs and traditions. Regardless of where we stand on this topic, our children *will* learn the new culture. Especially if our children are born here, we need to learn to respect the fact that they will not grow up as we did. They are largely raised in the new culture, and accept many mainstream values as their own.

Within the family, the differences between parents' cultural values and their children's cultural values can cause stress. We do better when we learn to expect these differences and manage them as we would any other family stress. Our children learn our cultural norms and expectations, but they are surrounded by those of their schoolmates. Cecilia, a social worker, describes some of the stresses she experienced as an adult:

> ■ ■ ■ *I grew up in a small town in Ecuador. My father was a good man and a town leader, but he ran a very strict household. He was one of the most respected people in town. He had a reputation to maintain, and that meant we had to maintain that reputation too. For example, all ten of us children were to have bathed before breakfast, be well groomed, and be seated awaiting him at exactly 7 a.m. before school. We were not to talk at the table, were to exhibit perfect manners at all times, were to follow his instructions, and were to ask for advice on all important matters.*
>
> *Well, he sent me off to the United States for college at age eighteen. I stayed, got an advanced degree, developed a professional career, acquired citizenship, and some dozen years later was able to move my parents and some of my siblings here to join me. What a shock! I had been on my own, a successful woman making my own decisions and planning my own life. My parents were proud of my accomplishments, but suddenly my father wanted to know everywhere I was going, and he wanted to tell me what to do—in my own house. I did not realize how much I had changed. If I had*

*stayed in Ecuador and lived with my parents, I might have accepted this. As a career woman accustomed to independence, it was simply not possible, no matter how much I loved my father and wanted to respect his wishes.* ■ ■ ■

When our children are younger, solutions can be challenging. For example, for some of us, it would have been unheard of that a playmate from school would invite one of us over for a "slumber party." Yet these are quite common in the United States. What are good parents to do when their ten-year-old daughter is invited to a slumber party with her girlfriends from school? We want her to fit in and enjoy her friends. If we follow the way we were raised, we would say "no." In fact, the invitation would never have occurred! It can be hard to know what the friend's parents are like, and we can't monitor our child at someone else's house. This is a problem for our children too.

There is no one right answer to such problems. But the reality is that our children will learn from and adopt values and beliefs that are at least a little different than our own. Some may choose paths that favor much more independence and individualism than we would like. As adults, we can still have very wonderful relationships with our children. But during the difficult middle years, we may be frustrated by the way they challenge our authority. It can also trouble us when our children go to college, move out, and start their own families. Some research has found that young people aged 23 to 26 have the most conflicts with their parents about issues of acculturation. These conflicts have some negative impact. For example, they are associated with increased depression and lower self-esteem among the younger generations.[15]

Parents also acculturate at different rates. This can be quite difficult when the children are acculturated and one parent is acculturated but the other is less so. The children may tend to side with the acculturated parent, and that can create discord in the marriage.[16]

In some families, an unsettling role reversal occurs. The children learn English quickly and are better able to navigate new systems. They take over some responsibilities that should fall to the adults. Parents end up depending on their children's skills. Parents find themselves feeling powerless and insignificant, and children are put in a position of making decisions that they are not mentally prepared to make. In some cases, children may not tell their parents the full story, so parents can't appropriately discipline their children. (This is one reason it is critical that immigrants enroll in English language courses.)

Santiago is a forty-five-year-old engineer who was born in Puerto Rico but has raised his children in North Dakota. He had an eye-opening moment when he helped during a school field trip:

▪▪▪ *As Puerto Ricans, we are U.S. citizens, yet people still ask if I'm a citizen. That has always bothered me. But I recently learned that it's even stranger for my children. They were born where we live now, in North Dakota. If you were to talk to them on the phone, you'd hear that clipped accent that native North Dakotans have. You'd never guess their parents were Puerto Ricans. It's cold and flat and not that green here. It's about as far as you can get from the feeling of Puerto Rico. And yet people still ask my kids where they are from just because of the way they look.*

*Recently I helped with a school field trip and had time to watch my children interact with all the other children. We speak Spanish at home and we try to eat favorite foods from our mothers' recipes—at least, whenever we can find produce that will work. But watching my children talk with and be with the other schoolchildren opened my eyes. I realized that my children were living in two worlds. On the field trip, they acted more like their schoolmates than like their mother and me. For a moment, I could have been watching someone else's children. That was when I realized that they had to navigate one world at school, with their friends, and then navigate our "imported" Puerto Rican world at home. I thought about how hard that would be, and I came to respect my children in a new way. It also helped me understand them a bit better.* ▪▪▪

Children are aware of the differences, too. They may be concerned that parents stereotype them based on the way they are dressed, for example, when the child is simply trying to fit in with his peers at school. Latino children, when questioned about the impact of the difference in acculturation between them and their parents, describe some of the difficult issues. One child said, "Being here, [there are] a lot of different types of people you hang around with. And then your parents, they don't know that. They don't know what you have to do to fit in with certain people and stuff like that. So when you try to talk to them about it, it [is] kind of weird. Because they don't understand." Another child pointed out, "You can get pressure by kids to act different when you're not used to it ... so you can feel distant [from your parents] sometimes."[17]

One of the losses we feel with these differences is that our families don't seem quite as close as we wish. They probably are *not* as close as the family we grew up with, but we are in a different place and a different time. We can't bring what was in the past into the present: *Lo que ha pasado es pasado*. The memories that we had, and the vision that we have, may have to change to fit the new circumstances. The freedom and independence that our young people accept as new values may worry us. They want to go out with their friends, and we worry that they may use alcohol or other drugs, get into trouble, or make stupid mistakes that would reflect badly on them and us. These are legitimate worries. But freedom and independence are tied to opportunity, education, job advancement, and other benefits that we hope our children will obtain. We and our children have to balance these values.

### Families and relationships hurt by immigration

In many cases, a family is split up by immigration. For example, one person comes to the United States to build up enough savings to send back and bring more of the family. Or perhaps the whole family immigrates, but later, one member is deported and the others stay in the United States. These splits are devastating to the family.

First, people change while they are apart. This is especially true for the person or people from the family who come to the new culture first. They have been here longer and have had a longer time to adapt, adjust, and acculturate. Then when the rest of the family comes, they have unequal knowledge, and this creates some stress.

Second, during a time of separation, both partners in a relationship become lonely. Despite their best intentions, relationships outside of the primary one can occur. This is a tough problem that can be helped by counseling. Not every family has problems. Some do have problems, yet find a way to reconcile and reintegrate. And some families simply have to part ways. The loss of a relationship and the fracturing of a family creates many practical problems. Caring for children becomes more difficult. Single parents become exhausted, and it sometimes may be harder for them to maintain discipline and help the children with all of their needs. Often the split diminishes the family income.

But just as important, the loss of a relationship is a cause of grief. We enter into relationships with dreams of the future. When love dies and a relationship falls apart, we can feel overwhelmed with grief. This may be true even when both partners are better off as the result of a split, because both still suffer the loss of a dream. The support of our families, friends, and communities, sometimes accompanied by counseling, can help us recover from the grief.

After a split, the person who is no longer with the children usually is required to pay child support. This can be frustrating for both former partners. A man may think, "She has the children and is now living with another man. Why must I send money to her?" The support is for the children, and this is why it must be paid—to support them. Even if he receives all his wages in cash, the father is still required to help support the children. And if the children are living with the father, then the mother must help support the children. Both partners need to develop a means of communicating civilly after the split. Fathers are just as important as mothers when rearing children, and for this reason, parents who no longer live together need to find ways to be sure the children see both parents, unless one of them is dangerous to the children.

**Violence in the home**

In chapter 3, we will discuss how traumatic events affect our emotional life. In this chapter, we will explore the trauma of violence in the home. Physical and emotional abuse, sexual abuse, neglect, and domestic violence can do great harm to a family.

*Domestic violence* is generally viewed as physically or emotionally violent behavior between spouses. *Neglect* and *physical, emotional,* and *sexual abuse* occur when appropriate care is ignored or withheld or whenever a vulnerable person is harmed physically, emotionally, or sexually by a caregiver. All children are vulnerable, as are people who are mentally or physically unable to defend themselves, such as older adults and those who are impaired.

Neglect or abuse is never acceptable. However, in some of our regions of origin, some degree of physical punishment was used, and there may have been no penalties for other kinds of violence. In our home region, the law may have ignored events such as a parent beating a child, a man beating his wife, or a man having sexual relations with an underage person, even if these practices were considered wrong and immoral. In the United States, there are strong legal consequences for these events. Even if a person has grown up with parents who used harsh punishments in their country of origin, those actions are not acceptable here.

### Child abuse

Antonia was shocked when the authorities came to her home to meet with her late in the afternoon. She learned there had been a report that one of her children had been physically abused by her husband. As it turned out, her husband had slapped the child hard across the face for being disobedient and disrespectful. At school the next day, the child showed up with a bruise in the shape of a hand on his face. The teacher sent the child to the administrator's office, where the staff had reported a suspected case of physical abuse.

The authorities waited for Antonia's husband to arrive home and talked to him. He was outraged that someone would come into his house and accuse him of not taking good care of his children. He had been raised with a strict hand, and he had turned out well! His children would be raised the same way. Who were these people trying to tell him how to run his house? His children would be better off if they learned to follow the rules.

Antonia and her husband were mandated to attend parenting classes at a local community center. There they learned some new ways to discipline their children.

Child abuse is the physical, sexual, or emotional maltreatment or neglect of a child. These events may occur at home, but they may also occur elsewhere—at a relative's house, at church, or at school, for example.

Child physical abuse involves any physical aggression that an adult directs at a child. This includes infliction of bruises, scratches, cuts, burns, broken bones, or other rough treatment that could harm the child. Babies who are shaken as a form of punishment or because of the parent's frustration are also considered physically abused.

Child emotional abuse involves loud yelling, name-calling, ridicule, humiliation, cruel treatment, harsh criticism, and other nonphysical attempts to denigrate the child.

Child sexual abuse occurs when an adult or older adolescent abuses a child for sexual stimulation. Besides rape or forced sexual conduct, making a child undress, showing the child pornographic material, or forcing the child to pose for pornographic photos or videos constitutes sexual abuse.

Child neglect occurs when a parent or other caregiver does not provide the child with needed food, clothing, shelter, medical care, or supervision to such a degree that the child's well-being is threatened. Neglect also includes lack of appropriate attention to the child.

These events can physically damage the child in the present, but often the tragedy extends far into the future. Some children who have experienced these forms of abuse have a greater risk of psychiatric problems. They may experience anxiety, depression, post-traumatic stress disorder, and other challenges for decades, or even their entire lives. In addition to the immediate damages done, long-term physical damage can include brain damage (when head trauma occurs or when a baby is shaken), poor or slowed development, and impaired brain development.

It can be difficult to know when a child is being abused. We may see changes in mood and behavior, changes in eating or sleeping habits, changes in school performance and attendance, lack of personal care or hygiene, or risk-taking behaviors.

In the United States, when an authority suspects that a child (or other vulnerable person) is being abused or neglected, the authority is required to report the suspected abuse. The child will be interviewed, and so will the people who are suspected of perpetrating the abuse. Authorities will decide what sort of assistance the child and family needs and be sure that it is provided. Perpetrators may face legal consequences. When parents or caregivers are the perpetrators, they may be required to attend parenting classes to help them improve their parenting, although the consequences may be much more severe than that.

---

### Help for child abuse

If you suspect that a child has been abused, you can call the **National Child Abuse Hotline** at **1-800-422-4453** (1-800-4-A-CHILD). Crisis counselors are available twenty-four hours a day, seven days a week. You can also visit the website at www.childhelp.org. The counselors can help if you

- are in physical or emotional crisis
- need to find local assistance
- need to know the signs of child abuse
- need to know how to report known or suspected abuse
- need to know what will happen if you report abuse
- seek information on programs that can help children
- simply need to talk

### *Domestic violence*

Domestic violence is a pattern of abusive behavior used by one person to gain or maintain control over an intimate partner. The pattern can include physical, sexual, emotional, economic, or psychological threats or actions targeting another person.[18] This might include hurting or trying to hurt a partner by hitting or kicking; forcing a partner to take part in an unwanted, nonconsensual sexual act; threatening physical or sexual violence; threatening a person's loved ones or possessions; or harming the person's sense of self-worth.

It is never acceptable for people in a relationship to strike each other or abuse each other emotionally. Even though we may have observed such behavior in our parents' generation, that behavior should not continue. *Con un error no se subsana otro.* It is not acceptable to repeat the actions of our parents when their actions were wrong, but we can understand that perhaps they were not taught a better way.

Domestic violence damages the victim in many ways. In the United States, some three women are killed by domestic violence every day, and many more suffer minor or major injuries. Victims may have emotional trauma symptoms, such as flashbacks, panic attacks, sleeping difficulties, depression, suicidal thoughts, difficulty trusting other people, and difficulty forming new intimate relationships. Sometimes victims of domestic violence try to cope with their trauma in unproductive ways, such as using alcohol or other drugs or having risky sex.[19]

Usually women are the victims of domestic violence, although in some cases, men are the victims. It can happen in heterosexual and same-sex couples, across all ages, ethnic backgrounds, and economic levels.

Domestic violence also tears apart the family. Children who live in families under the influence of domestic violence have an increased risk of social and physical problems. They learn that violence is a normal way of life, and that increases the risk that they will teach another generation that violence is acceptable. Let's look at Marisol's situation.

■■■ *Marisol loved her man. He could be tender and loving, and he was handsome. She held down two jobs, and he stayed at home, hanging with his friends and smoking pot, but she loved him anyway. He would complain that she didn't keep house right, that her cooking was bad, that she was getting fat, or that she looked at other men. He said these things in private and in front of other people, humiliating her. Sometimes Marisol felt she was walking on eggshells, fearing his anger. Something would set him off, he would explode like an overinflated balloon, and he would beat her. Sometimes, she knew he was going to explode, so she did something to provoke him, just to get the beating over with. Afterward, he was always tender and loving, and she felt things would get better. But at work, her friends noticed. The bruises on her arms told them what was going on. "You should leave that guy. He's no good," they would say.* ■■■

It can be hard to understand why a person like Marisol would not try to leave a relationship in which she is being assaulted. When there are children, it can be just as damaging for them to see the violence done against their parent. Victims are often afraid of more problems if they report the assault. They may fear losing their children or fear that they won't be believed. Other members of the family may try to discourage the person from reporting the violence. Victims may have grown up in similar households and think that humiliation and violence are part of being in a relationship, or that they deserved it. If the family includes children, the victim may believe in keeping the family together despite personal harm, not realizing that the violence is also harming the children.

In the United States, laws help the victims of domestic violence get protection through the legal system. There are shelters for victims of domestic violence and programs to help the survivors of violence recover from trauma and other issues. Some programs can help partners stay safe while planning to leave an abusive relationship. There are also treatment programs designed to help abusers break the cycle of violence.

Domestic abuse is bad for the family. People who are experiencing such abuse can get the help they need to develop a safety plan for themselves and their children and to resolve the situation so no one is hurt again.

## Breaking the pattern of abuse

Domestic violence is not acceptable. No one has the right to express anger violently or hurt another person. If you answer "yes" to any of these questions, you may be in an abusive relationship.

Does your partner

- embarrass you with put-downs?

- look at you or act in ways that scare you?

- control what you do, whom you see or talk to, or where you go?

- stop you from seeing your friends or family members?

- take your money or Social Security checks, make you ask for money, or refuse to give you money?

- make all of the decisions?

- tell you that you're a bad parent or threaten to take away or hurt your children?

You can call for help even if you are an undocumented person. Services available to you include domestic violence shelters, hospitals, legal aid, and counseling and support groups. You should call the police for help, ask them to complete a report, and leave the house with your children and important papers.[20]

To learn more about your options, call the **National Domestic Violence Hotline** at **1-800-799-7233** (TTY 1-800-787-3224).

For more information on domestic violence, see www.thehotline.org. Many of the resources there are available in Spanish.

## Summary: Chapter 2—Family

Whatever country we come from, almost all Latinos value spirituality and extended family. Our families are a great source of support and mental well-being. But here in the United States, we may find different conditions for family life. For example, if both parents must work, or one parent must work two jobs, some of our expectations may be impossible to meet. Our children learn English and learn to navigate the systems here more rapidly than we do. The stresses of immigration can also create troubles for a family. Sometimes it seems that everything is flipped upside down!

Despite these troubles, most Latinos find ways to enjoy their family life. Family plays an important role in our own mental health. Learning to communicate with our partners and children, and to maintain positive discipline at home is important to family well-being. Child abuse and domestic abuse disrupt many families but there are people who can help us with these problems if we suspect they are occurring. Our elders have a very important role in our families and helping them to live good, long lives makes our family stronger.

Questions to think about:

- What is family to me? Who is part of my family? How does my family make me a stronger person?
- What is the role of elders in my family?
- What do my family and I think about acting differently from our traditional family roles after arriving in the United States?

### *Reflection questions*

1. Are our actions, decisions, and thoughts contributing to or working against our family purpose and goals?
2. What "rules" do we think people should follow to be a good man or a good woman in the family? For each of these rules, where did we learn this rule? Who benefits from the rule? Does the rule make sense in the place we live now and in the economic conditions we face? Is this rule fair?

3. What is family to me? Who is part of my family? How does my family make me a stronger person?

4. Is more than one culture represented within my family? How do I navigate cultural differences in my family?

5. Do I communicate with relatives in a respectful manner? When considering differences from my ways of thinking, am I truly listening, trying to understand, and considering the other perspectives?

6. What is the role of elders in my family? What have I learned from my grandparents or elderly parents? How do I prepare to provide the best care I possibly can for a relative in advanced age?

7. Where can I go to find support when multiple family responsibilities put heavy demands on me?

8. What do my family and I think about acting differently from our traditional family roles after arriving in the United States?

9. Whether I'm following traditional roles or breaking tradition, how do I know whether I'm doing the right thing?

10. If my family and I separated in the process of immigration, what can I do to feel connected to them?

11. What else do I need to learn about the developmental stages my children will go through? What style of discipline did I learn growing up? What style of discipline do I use with my children? How do I know when I should ask for help with my parenting skills?

12. How do I help my children grow up feeling safe and confident?

13. Do I know the laws where I live about child abuse?

14. Do I know the laws where I live about domestic violence?

15. Do I know my child's teacher and how my child is doing in school?

## Resumen: Capítulo 2—Familia

Sin importar de qué país vengan, la mayoría de los latinos valoran la espiritualidad y la familia incluyendo los parientes lejanos. Nuestras familias son una excelente fuente de apoyo y bienestar mental. Pero en los Estados Unidos, podemos encontrar diferentes condiciones de vida familiar. Por ejemplo, si el padre y la madre deben trabajar, o uno de ellos tiene dos empleos, algunas de nuestras expectativas pueden ser imposibles de realizar. Nuestros hijos aprenden el inglés y entienden el sistema de este país más rápidamente que nosotros los adultos. Además, el estrés de la inmigración puede crear problemas para la familia. ¡A veces nos parece que todo está al revés! A pesar de esos problemas, la mayoría de los latinos encuentran la forma de disfrutar de la vida en familia. La familia juega un rol importante en nuestra salud mental. Aprender a comunicarnos con nuestros padres, con nuestros hijos, y mantener una disciplina positiva en el hogar es importante para el bienestar de la familia. El abuso infantil y el abuso doméstico trastorna a muchas familias, pero existen personas que pueden ayudarnos con esos problemas, si sospechamos que ocurren. Los ancianos tiene un rol importante en nuestras familias y ayudarles a mantenerse sanos y vivir largas vidas fortalece la familia.

Preguntas para reflexionar:

- ¿Qué significa la familia para mí? ¿Quién forma parte de mi familia? ¿Cómo mi familia me hace una persona más fuerte?
- ¿Cuál es el rol de los ancianos en mi familia?
- ¿Qué piensa mi familia cuando actuo diferente de mi rol tradicional después de llegar a los Estados Unidos?

CHAPTER

···three···

# Emotions in Harmony

Chapter 3 is about our emotions and how we can bring our emotions into harmony within ourselves and with other people. Many of us are unaware of why we react to certain situations the way we do. This chapter provides information and tools that help us understand how our emotions work. That understanding can help us find the harmony we seek. In this chapter, you will learn about these topics:

- what emotions are and some of the ways they affect us
- why it is important to name and talk about emotions
- how social and personal expectations shape our emotions
- some of the sources of our emotional responses and emotional patterns
- what traumatic events are and how they shape our emotional responses
- how stress affects our ability to cope with challenges and difficult emotions
- emotions in relationships
- things we can do to care for ourselves when we are upset emotionally
- common emotional illnesses and their symptoms
- how counselors can help you find harmony

MATÍAS AND LUPE WALK INTO A ROOM. Matías exclaims, "This room is too hot! Open a window!"

Lupe is aghast. "Too hot? You must be feverish. Everyone knows that this room is too cold. Somebody get me a sweater!"

Who is correct—Lupe or Matías? If you place a thermometer in the room, it will read the same temperature regardless of who looks at it. So again, who is correct?

Of course, we all know the answer to this question. Both are correct, because each person feels temperature in his or her own way.

Our emotions are just like our perceptions of hot and cold. What we feel is just *what we feel*. One feeling is not more correct than another. This may seem like a simple example, but let's push it a little further. If Lupe were in the room alone, temperature would not be a problem. She could make the room warmer and no one would mind. And if Matías were in the room alone, he could simply open a window and feel cooler. But they are in the room together, *so they are in conflict over their feelings about the room.*

We Latinos, in general, place a high value on *simpatía* — on *harmony*. We want to be in agreement with the people we love, with the community around us, and within ourselves. This is not an easy task! We can't help that our perceptions of hot and cold are different. It creates conflict, though, and conflict disrupts harmony. In exactly the same way, our emotional responses to the very same event can put us in conflict with each other and with ourselves. Understanding emotions can make it easier to obtain the harmony we desire.

In this chapter, you will learn some basic facts about emotions and emotional health that will help you find harmony:

- what emotions are and some of the ways they affect us
- why it is important to name and talk about emotions

- how social and personal expectations shape our emotions
- some of the sources of our emotional responses and emotional patterns
- what traumatic events are and how they shape our emotional responses
- how stress affects our ability to cope with challenges and difficult emotions
- emotions in relationships
- things we can do to care for ourselves when we are upset emotionally
- common emotional illnesses and their symptoms
- how counselors can help you find harmony

### Emotions

Imagine that you are hiking alone in the countryside. You have never been out so far before. You are enjoying the path under your feet, the scent of flowers in the air, the lovely landscape, the clouds rolling by, and the strong breeze. Then you hear a small crack—maybe a stick breaking in a grove of trees behind you.

You become instantly alert and aware. You turn swiftly, and behind you in the dark behind the trees, you see a panther. Now your alertness turns to fear. Your heart races. Your eyes grow wide. You sense that your life is in danger. You become extremely alert, and your muscles are tensed, ready to run or fight.

The breeze blows again and suddenly you see it—not a panther at all but a bit of fabric caught on a limb. You feel instant relief, maybe even a bit foolish. Your heartbeat and breathing slow. You feel happy to be alive! You register the information, too, so that next time maybe you won't be so quick to think the breeze and a scrap of fabric are the same thing as a panther.

When we experience emotions, we feel them inside us as facts. What we feel, *feels real*. Our body and our brains prepare us to act according to the emotional messages we recieve. In the panther example, the primary emotion was fear. And fear can be a good thing, enabling us to survive real panther attacks and much more. A bit of fear can protect us. If that scrap of fabric had really been a panther, your body would have been ready to run, climb, or even fight back.

But too much fear can make us sick. It can put us out of harmony. With fear, as with other emotions, when you have a better understanding of what is going on, you can do a better job of responding appropriately to outside events. You will have a better path to harmony.

Observe a baby or a young child, and you will see that they assume their emotions are facts. They also think that everyone around them has the same "facts." Young children are not aware that mother or father will not feel the same things. But of course, as children mature, they see that different people feel different emotions about the very same event.

This is like Lupe and Matías feeling the temperature in the room differently. Or imagine how an experienced guide who knew there were no panthers in the countryside would have reacted to the very same scene in the trees. She might have turned calmly to see what caused the noise, but she would not have been frightened by the breeze and a bit of fabric.

Our emotions are facts *about how we react to what we perceive.* These emotional facts are not the same thing as the facts of the world around us. This is how two or ten or thirty people can all have very different feelings about the very same event. Even as adults, our first reaction is generally to feel that our personal emotions are the only or best way to react to what we have just seen. It takes a moment for us to gain control and temper our personal emotional experience with other kinds of information.

The ways in which we perceive the world are shaped by many things:

- *Our experiences in childhood.* For example, an adult who as a child was attacked by a large dog may always feel threatened by large dogs. An adult who as a child loved and was loved by a large dog may always love large dogs. As adults, they both know that most dogs are friendly and a few are dangerous, but their immediate emotional responses to a large dog will always be different.

- *The things we believe or have been taught to believe.* A man who believes men must never be afraid is going to be angry at himself if he thinks a bit of fabric in the breeze is a panther. He may also feel embarrassed and try to hide his reaction from other people. But a man who believes it is acceptable for men to feel fear might laugh at himself for seeing a scrap of fabric as a panther, and he might entertain his friends by telling the story about how he was terrified by a bit of cloth.

- *The nature of our physical body.* Scientists do not know why, but some people are simply born more sensitive than other people to some kinds of experiences. Some people are more prone to feeling depression than others. Some are more prone to becoming alcoholics or drug addicts. Some people have much greater difficulty changing from one emotion to another. This is why even though a platoon of soldiers caught in a horrific battle can all come home physically uninjured, some will feel no ill effects from the battle, some will feel bad for a while but get better soon, and some will have deep, long-lasting emotional difficulties for many years.

- *Physical disorders that affect brain chemistry.* We now know that, in some ways, the human body is like a great chemistry set. The chemicals help convey messages about our inner and outer worlds. Sometimes chemical imbalances occur and can trigger emotional reactions that are not appropriate to the events around us.

- *Our physical condition at the moment an event occurs.* A person who is exhausted from working two jobs has a different reaction to the same event than a person who just woke up after a good night's sleep.

- *Our habitual emotional responses.* The way we tend to react can become like a well-worn path in the woods. If we always react to a large dog by feeling fear, it is as though the path to fear is the path of least resistance. We will react fearfully even after we've learned we don't need to be afraid. (Fortunately, just as we can create a new path in the woods, we can create a path to a new emotional reactions in our brains.)

Although our emotions and habitual responses are very useful in helping us deal with the world, sometimes they impede our success and happiness. We know they are getting in the way, but we can't change them. That is when talking to someone we trust is especially helpful. Sometimes that means talking with a trained spiritual counselor or therapist who helps people with emotions. Later in this chapter we discuss how therapy can help. But first let's explore more about emotions.

### *Learning to name emotions*

A person who has never seen or heard of an elephant and sees one for the first time can't tell you what he has seen. It is like a horse, but bigger. It has a nose like a snake. It is gray. Its ears look like giant leaves flapping in the breeze. When the person learns the name for elephant, we can say "elephant," and he will instantly see one in his mind's eye. Once he knows what an elephant is, he can talk about it with other people, learn more about it, ask questions, and be even better at understanding the kinds of elephants there are, how they live, where they live, and so forth.

Our emotions are similar. They are as rich and varied as the colors of the world. If we can't name them, though, we have trouble talking about them. And if we can't talk about them, we can't understand them. Many people have a great deal of trouble naming and talking about emotions.

"Some of my clients, men in particular, can name only two emotions—anger and happiness. Other clients, especially adolescents, have a great deal of trouble separating one emotion from another," said one counselor who helps people regain their sense of emotional harmony.

As Latinos, especially as newer immigrants, many of us (though not all) grew up in families with very traditional practices. In these families, the man was always the breadwinner and the head of the household. He set the rules and planned the family's path. He was responsible and hardworking. He helped us understand what our family and community could expect of us—our duties to family and society. The woman was the emotional head of the house. She was the one who nurtured and provided love. She helped bring arguments into harmony. She was the one we could confide in.

Because they are often raised this way, women tend to have greater familiarity with the emotional part of their lives than men do. Even though both men and women have the same natural capacity to experience and express many different emotional states, women may generally be better able to express emotions and talk about them because of the expectations they were raised with. Regardless of the reasons, some men have more difficulty than women when it comes to describing their emotions.

Sometimes, too, both men and women can become afraid of expressing their emotions. For example, if the only time we have observed emotions is when people are angry or violent, we may fear expressing our own anger. Or we may believe that the *only* way to express anger is to be physically or verbally violent.

Just like the person who now knows that the large gray animal with a snake-like nose and ears like giant leaves is an elephant, any person can learn to name their emotions and distinguish among their many "flavors." Gaining that vocabulary makes it easier to talk about feelings. Talking about our feelings helps us gain control over them. For example, the man who tries never to get angry because he is afraid that his anger may turn into violence can learn to put aside that fear by talking about the anger. As he talks about it, its power over him diminishes. He gains control over it rather than letting it have control over him.

The "many flavors of emotion" chart shows emotions in a way that helps you learn to name and understand them. Notice that at the center of the circle are six basic emotions:

- scared
- joyful
- powerful
- peaceful
- sad
- mad

Most of us can easily identify whether our most basic feeling is like one of these. We know when we feel scared, for example. But what *kind* of scared do we feel? Just as one can taste many flavors of salsa—sweet and mild, savory and rich, salty and hot—we can distinguish many shades of fear.

From scared, if you move out one ring around the circle, you will find more flavors of emotion, all related to the feeling of being scared:

- confused
- rejected
- helpless
- submissive
- insecure
- anxious

Confused, rejected, helpless, submissive, insecure, anxious— each flavor of fear is a little different.

The outermost circle helps add yet another specific touch of flavor to the basic flavor. So we know that feeling discouraged can be a form of feeling rejected, which itself can be a form of being scared.

Let's consider a story that shows how untangling confused emotions helps a family find harmony. Meet Alicia and her son Eduardo.

### Clarifying our emotions: One family's story

Alicia showed up at a family help center with her teenage son, Eduardo. She was at her wit's end. She had left her small village in Bolivia ten years earlier, a single mother who wanted to earn enough money to make a better life for her son. Her son had been cared for in Bolivia by aunts and uncles and grandparents. She had called as often as she could afford to, and as she gradually saved money, she called even more often and sent money home to help with his education and to help the rest of her family too. Finally, she had saved enough money to bring him to live with her. By this time he was fifteen years old.

At first Eduardo was happy to see her. He cried and hugged her, and she cried too. For the first time, he met his younger brother and sister, who had been born in the United States some years after his mother had moved here. For the first few weeks, he was happy to have his mother back, to have a new brother and sister, and to have a home to stay in.

Soon, though, his moods began to swing. He would be very quiet and look darkly at his mother. Then he would say disrespectful things and disobey her. He would stay out at night, or he would argue with his younger brother and sister. When Alicia asked Eduardo what was going on, he couldn't or wouldn't tell her. He began to find power in being silent, ignoring her questions and her attempts to bring harmony to her family. Finally he began threatening to run away and live on the street or find a way back to Bolivia.

Alicia could not understand what was going on. From the moment she had left Bolivia, she had put her energy into reuniting her family—and look at how she was being treated! After she and a counselor talked for a while, she agreed that Eduardo could talk to the counselor alone.

The counselor asked Eduardo what he was feeling. Was he mad? Happy? Scared? At first, Eduardo could not talk. He said he loved his mother and knew he should feel happy that he could finally be with her. He knew she loved him. But he felt all mixed up inside.

Eduardo was confused, which is normal, especially for adolescents. The counselor helped Eduardo sort through his feelings. They looked at the wheel of feelings—the same "many flavors of emotion" chart that appears in this chapter. Eduardo found a lot of feelings that described what was going on inside—feelings besides confusion.

He and the counselor talked during several visits. As Eduardo used the chart, he became better able to talk about what was going on. He became less confused. He soon was able to say that he felt these emotions:

- helpless about being in a new place and leaving his old home
- joyful and excited to be reunited with his mother and to finally meet his brother and sister
- hurt, angry, hostile, and rejected because his mother had left him behind for so many years
- isolated because his brother and sister and mother were all so familiar with each other; they had many friends but he had none
- excited to be in a new place with many new things to learn
- insecure because he did not feel comfortable and could not speak the language
- inadequate because in his old home he was very confident and could do anything in the village, but in his new home he "felt like a baby" and did not understand anything
- embarrassed because he felt he should be able to control his emotions, but they were overpowering him, and because he kept disrespecting his mother even though he did not want to
- guilty and ashamed because he believed he should be grateful for all his mother had done and for the opportunity to reunite with his family, but instead he felt angry and jealous
- confused because he wanted to feel happy but had all these other feelings

The more Eduardo and his counselor talked, the more comfortable Eduardo became having so many feelings at once. Finally, the counselor invited Alicia back into the counseling sessions, and Eduardo and Alicia talked. He was able to tell his mother things he had been feeling. They began to talk openly. After several more visits, Eduardo was no longer so confused. His feelings were settling down. He began obeying his mother. He assumed his responsibility as the oldest brother to set a positive example for his younger siblings. He enrolled in school and began to feel like a member of his new household.

Alicia, meanwhile, came to understand that Eduardo was not the baby she'd left behind; he was becoming a man and needed to be more independent. As he showed that he was able to be responsible, she gave him more freedoms and did not hover about him so much.

Alicia still brings Eduardo in to see the counselor from time to time. Mostly, though, their problems are the typical problems that happen between a teenager and a parent—problems that can be resolved through communication. These are complicated by Eduardo learning a new language, navigating a new set of expectations, wanting to make new friends and explore his new neighborhood, and feeling changes in his own maturing body. But they are no worse than other problems, and Eduardo's experience of sorting through his confused emotions has equipped him to cope with the challenges he will face in the future.

It would be easy for a person looking from the outside to say that Eduardo was simply being a disrespectful boy because he would not follow the rules, or to say that Alicia was failing as a mother by not making Eduardo comply. But that's the thing about feelings. No matter what we believe *should* happen, feelings seem to have a life of their own. Maturity and wisdom come as we learn to name and talk about our feelings and gain a deeper understanding of where they come from.

### External expectations shape emotions

External expectations shape our emotional well-being. For example, many people have well-defined expectations about the attributes of an ideal man and an ideal woman, about how a family should look and behave, and about how people should treat one another. Some of these expectations come from their religion, their culture, and their parents. These social forces affect us constantly. Some we reject, but others we accept, embrace, and internalize. They become personal expectations.

These expectations set boundaries around which emotional responses are considered acceptable and which are not. These expectations can add to the confusion we face when trying to understand our emotions. Often these expectations are hidden from us.

## Many Flavors of Emotion

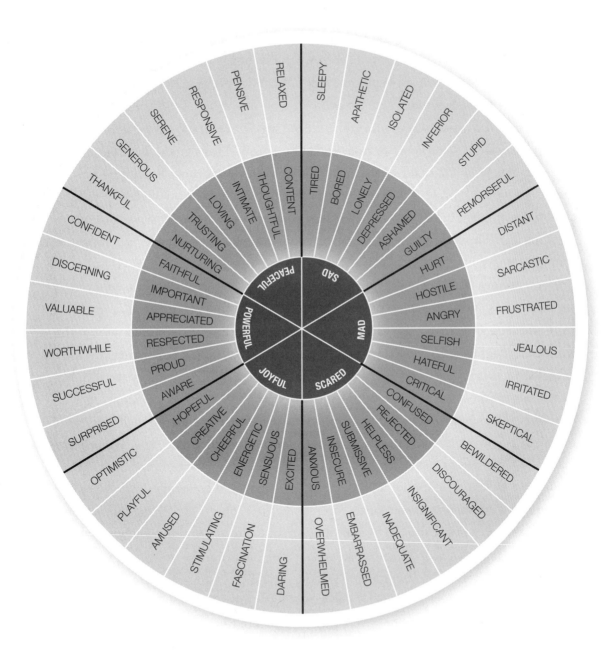

Source: Adapted from "The Feeling Wheel: A Guide to Your Feelings,"
© 2000 by Christopher Cobb.

They are like a stone buried in the path—we may stub our toe on the surface, but the rest of the stone is hidden deep in the ground. The best way to avoid stubbing our toe again is to dig up the stone. We can also dig up and examine our expectations about feelings and behaviors—whether social or personal. Doing so helps us understand and perhaps change the ones that aren't helpful. Even if we don't change them, at least the decision to follow them will be *ours,* not someone else's. When we become aware of the expectations, the emotions they cause may change.

For example, some cultures and families have strong expectations that a "real" man never feels afraid. So when a man from such a background feels afraid, he is faced with other emotions too. He will feel ashamed that he feels fear, because his culture says he should not be afraid. He may feel he needs to hide his emotion, even though talking about the fear might help him overcome it. He may feel angry because he is unable to express his fear. This shows how social expectations complicate and shape our emotional responses. A normal reaction of fear becomes tainted with shame and anger. If he has to suppress feelings of fear often, he may become very anxious or defensive. He may even lash out angrily at others just to prove to himself that he is not afraid.

Consider another example—a woman who is faced with social expectations that she will always happily sacrifice everything for her parents, siblings, and children. She may be in deep need of something for herself, but she feels a social pressure to sacrifice her own needs for those of others. This pressure can make her feel other emotions, such as resentment of those people for whom she sacrifices, jealousy of those in the family who get what they want, and anger at a sense of unfairness. At the same time, she believes that she is supposed to feel happy by sacrificing her needs for those of her family—even though the sacrificing does not always make her happy and sometimes makes her unhappy. So her emotions become confused. If she has to suppress her feelings about making such sacrifices often, she can become anxious or depressed without knowing why.

We saw this confusion when we learned about Eduardo, the young man recently reunited with his mother. Eduardo believed he should feel happy and grateful, but he felt helpless, jealous, and angry. The conflict between his beliefs about what he should feel and his actual feelings made it very difficult for him to talk with his mother about his feelings.

Remember, these expectations are often buried underground. We only know they are there when, as with the stone in our path, we stub our toe on them. For example, the man feeling fear may not even realize that he is worried about showing fear, and the woman may not know she is angry about sacrificing herself all the time. But emotions always find a way to come out. If we don't bring them out, they can make us miserable—and other people, too.

Just as it helps to learn the many flavors of emotion so we can talk about them, it helps to understand the way social expectations shape how we express our emotions. The more we understand these expectations, the more we can make choices about whether they contribute to our happiness. We can change or modify our behavior, and our emotional responses may begin to change too.

Every emotion has a place. When seeking harmony, we need to do the following:

- learn to understand the broad range of emotions that we have
- learn to understand what causes our emotional responses
- learn to express our emotions safely and in ways consistent with the situation that faces us
- learn how to communicate about our emotions while recognizing the constraints of our social and personal expectations

### *Emotional habits*

Earlier we learned that some events repeatedly trigger the same emotional responses from us. Like a well-worn path through the woods, a certain reaction "kicks in" in response to certain kinds of events, even when that reaction does not fit the circumstances and does not contribute to our own well-being.

We can observe this in animals. For example, a dog will come running the minute you begin to open a can because he associates that sound with being fed. The can opener is a trigger for his habit. We can develop good habits and bad habits—habits that bring happiness or bring unhappiness.

Think again of the person who was attacked by a dog as a child and is afraid of all dogs as a result. Every time he walks down the street, he encounters large dogs. If he reacts with fear to every dog, his heart will be racing all the time. He will feel miserable and may eventually quit going out in his neighborhood at all. His habit of reacting to dogs with fear is not good for his health or happiness.

We can learn new habits, though. For example, by getting to know a few friendly small dogs, and then some larger dogs, and eventually adopting a dog of his own, the man may learn a new emotional habit. He will no longer feel constrained by his fear.

Another way of describing a habit is as a pattern—something that repeats again and again. When something repeats over and over, we *expect* it to happen again. Some emotional patterns may be set very early in childhood. Imagine an adult who as a child was only surrounded by a family and community who always showed complete tenderness, love, and generosity for the child and for each other. That child, as an adult, will most likely expect all people to be kind in the same ways.

Now imagine a child raised in a different setting, where she only saw selfishness, had to fight for every scrap of food and bit of shelter, and saw that everyone around her had to do the same. As an adult, this person is more likely to believe that other people are a threat. Even if, as an adult, she moves into a community of people who are very generous, she will most likely expect even generous people to be selfish. She will probably be suspicious of their motives. Similarly, if the adult from the generous community moves into the selfish community, he will likely expect the people to be generous and will be continually surprised when they don't share, even if he does.

These extreme examples only serve to make a point. Most of us grow up with a mix of positive and negative experiences. Even though we have experiences that are disruptive, we have family who care about us, and they help us find our ways into adulthood. Nevertheless, things that happen to us in childhood shape our emotional responses— our habits or patterns—when we are adults. These things can stay hidden from us, but they continue to shape our responses to events and to the people we meet.

### Traumatic events

Certain kinds of early childhood and adolescent experiences can be extremely disruptive and can set obstacles in our path to future happiness. Counselors call experiences that have lasting harmful effects "traumatic events."

An event is traumatic when it overwhelms our capacity to respond. Think of the capacity to respond as a water glass. We can add only so much water to the glass before it will overflow. Just as some glasses can hold more water than others, some people naturally seem to have a larger capacity for coping with disruptive events than other people do. We don't fully understand why this is; psychologists are doing research to find out why. Early in this chapter, we described a group of soldiers who all went through the same horrific battle and all survived physically uninjured. Yet some came back from the war feeling normal while others experienced depression. Each soldier had his own, different capacity to survive the trauma.

Many kinds of traumatic events can happen to children, adolescents, and adults:

- experiencing violence
- witnessing violence perpetrated against someone else
- experiencing hunger and starvation
- being neglected—not having our physical or emotional needs looked after
- experiencing verbal abuse—for example, lots of shouting, name-calling, or threats of violence
- being forced to do things one knows are wrong
- experiencing sexual abuse

These experiences are traumatic and damaging—regardless of our age. But when they happen to children, and even to adolescents, they are more likely to create emotional patterns that thwart happiness. Children, and many adolescents, do not have the skills to talk about their feelings, and they lack the experience to see events in a greater context. They almost always feel that they somehow *caused* the bad thing that happened to them—although of course they did not. So when children experience traumatic events, they often bury them deep inside. These events can make the child feel ashamed, inferior, and secretive. Without knowing why, the child may behave in ways that cause problems with relationships and with the ability to feel normal. This behavior can persist into adulthood, making it more difficult for the adult to make choices that lead to happiness.

Some Latino immigrants have come to the United States to escape conditions that included traumatic events like those we've described. They may have fled unsafe regions with frequent violence, criminal activity, or other abuse that left them in a constant state of fear. They may have been left to fend for themselves at a very early age. Some arrive in the United States telling stories of extreme starvation as a child, of experiencing daily stomach pains and cramping, and of drifting to sleep worried about when they might eat again.

These events make us feel terrible as they happen, of course, but they also set emotional patterns that can lead to ongoing sadness, anxiety, or other emotional issues later in life. We may feel the events were somehow our fault, even though they were not. We may feel ashamed because we could not stop the events. We often try to bury them—to forget them. But they can erupt in unusual ways to affect our happiness and harmony. Cristina's story is one example.

### Haunted by the past: Cristina's story

Cristina had lived in the United States for almost ten years. She had arrived with her eighteen-month-old son to join her brother, sister, uncle, and several other family members who had immigrated earlier. She had established herself well and now, at age twenty-eight, had a reliable job and enough income to support herself and her son.

Shortly after her boy turned nine, Cristina began to have terrible nightmares. Sometimes, in her dreams, strange masked people tried to steal her child. Or she would see him swept away by a tornado or turning to dust when she went to hug and hold him. She would awake in a panic. At first she tried to ignore these dreams, but they persisted, and she often woke in the morning more tired than she had felt when she went to bed.

The dreams continued for months. They began to affect her waking activities. She became more fearful of letting her son out of her sight. Sometimes while at work, she could not concentrate, worried about what might happen to him at school. Sometimes she found ways to stay at home from work and keep him out of school because she was terrified of losing him. Finally, the principal of her son's elementary school called her to ask about his frequent absences from school: the absences might affect his promotion to the next grade. She asked Cristina what was wrong, since the boy seemed very healthy, and Cristina could not explain it. She could not explain her actions to the principal, and she could not explain them to herself. But she knew she was harming the well-being of her family. She felt she was failing in her duties as a mother. And she was growing sadder and was always tired. Sometimes she would cry for no reason.

That's when Cristina went to see a counselor. After several meetings, the counselor asked Cristina to tell the story of her arrival in the United States. It took her time to remember. She had forgotten most of it—her first memories were of great fear and everything seemed like a blur. What she did vaguely remember terrified her. She had crossed a long desert on foot with a guide and twelve other people, sleeping outside at night. Early one morning, the group awoke to find that one of the children was gone. The guide was an angry man who kept shouting at them to keep moving or he would leave them all alone. Still, the party searched for the lost girl for some time. They could not find her, and they finally moved on, all but the girl's father, who stayed behind to keep up the search, begging his wife to continue on with their other children.

Cristina's son at the time was unusually active. Sometimes he walked along with the group, but for the rest of the journey, she strapped him to her back and took him off only to feed or change him. She was terrified that he would wander off, too, so she slept very little, watching him all night. Meanwhile, she heard the missing child's mother weeping and thought about the child and her father, each searching alone in the desert. She worried constantly. Later the group heard that both the father and child were presumed dead. Cristina felt guilty and ashamed that she had not insisted everyone keep searching to save the child. But she had much to do to survive herself. So she blocked out the memory and got to work. She never told a soul what had happened, and she had gradually put it out of her mind. That was why it took so long to put the story back together.

When she told the story to her counselor, the counselor helped her see how this traumatic event was affecting her today, even though it had happened long ago. It wasn't just that she had become fearful and overly protective of her son. There were other things—she had refused to meet men that her family had suggested for her and she insisted she never wanted to have more children. She was afraid in wide-open spaces. She realized that she had not felt happy in ten years. Even in recent photos at family baptisms and parties, everyone was smiling—but her smile looked forced. Some part of her felt that she was a coward who would never be good enough. And because she was desperately afraid of losing her son, she had turned away from opportunities for him and for herself. She knew this was stunting her son's development, but she couldn't stop herself.

In time, Cristina worked with the counselor to understand the choices she had made to protect her son and herself, to forgive herself, and to be less controlling of her son. Her nightmares gradually diminished. She was able to share the story first with her son, who was old enough to understand, and later with her family. She began to smile, and was able to let her son experience the normal adventures a young person should.

Cristina was lucky to find a counselor and recall the terrifying experience that was creating her present-day unhappiness. Cristina was eighteen when her trauma occurred. When the trauma happens at a much earlier age it can be even harder to uncover and resolve, but resolution is always possible.

### Stress and coping capacity

The amount of daily stress we face affects our capacity to cope with frustrations and problems. It takes energy to face challenges. These challenges can come from outside us, such as difficulties finding work or getting transportation to a job. They may also come from within, such as the challenges of overcoming traumatic events.

Consider two people who each catch a cold with a cough. One of them has a well-paying job, good health care, healthy foods to eat, and a comfortable place to recuperate. The other person has to work two jobs and barely earns enough money, is physically exhausted, does not have a health care provider, and lives in his car. We are not surprised that the first one recovers from his cold and cough quickly, while the other one takes longer to heal. The second person has less capacity to cope with the cold and cough.

It is similar with emotional events. Many of us arrive in the United States already weary; we have traveled far, spent all our savings to get here, and must find work and a place to settle. We may have limited English skills, and some of us do not have immigration documents. This is very stressful. And if we are living as undocumented residents or have let our papers lapse, we live with daily fear of discovery. These stressors accumulate. The stress can reach a point where we are unable to cope well with the next new challenge. This makes us very vulnerable to strong feelings. We can be more irritable, find less humor in life, have more difficulty communicating with our families, or become angry with our children. We may shout and yell at our spouses or children without knowing why.

One common reaction to the accumulation of stress is that we disconnect from others, even our families. We isolate ourselves. In some cases, as with the story of Alicia, we isolate ourselves because we feel ashamed of our past, even if we can't easily recall the shameful event. In other cases, we isolate ourselves because we feel unsuccessful in our current activities. Many times, we are not even aware of how much we have isolated ourselves.

Just when we most need the sources of our greatest strength—our families, friends, and communities—we begin to pull away from them. This can create a vicious cycle. The more we pull away, the harder it is to talk to the people who can most help us cope. This is a good signal that outside help from a trusted counselor, minister, or elder would be useful.

### Emotions in relationships

Among the reasons people frequently give for coming to see a counselor are troubles in a family, marriage, or romantic relationship.

In relationships, the very thing that makes one person happy may make another person unhappy. Vicente is an artist who feels happiest when there is some clutter in the house, but Juanita is a health inspector who has been known to clean the back of the refrigerator with a toothbrush. Jorge is happy when his family and friends come over whenever they want and stay as late as they wish, but Maria is happy when she and Jorge are alone together.

Some of these problems can be worked out easily. But other problems in relationships go much deeper. Sometimes the differences are so great that they can't be resolved and the couple must part ways. Other times the couple can work together to find solutions that help both partners feel happy. Sometimes the problems they face are based in trauma they experienced earlier in their lives, as this couple learned.

### *Juliana and Ernesto's story*

Ernesto and Juliana were referred to a counselor after they had been in a serious fight. They were not even sure how the fight happened—but suddenly, there they were, screaming at each other, hitting each other, and breaking furniture. The neighbors had called the police, who stopped the fight, and a judge required that they go to counseling.

This was Juliana's second marriage. Her first husband had been truly cruel, beating and mistreating her, berating her in private and in front of family members, and constantly threatening her. She had endured the marriage for some years but finally escaped. She vowed then that no one would ever mistreat her again. For many years after that, she rarely dated. But one day she met Ernesto, a gentle, polite man, and after some years of friendship, they fell in love and eventually found an apartment together.

Ernesto was the youngest child in his family. He had grown up with an older brother who was a true bully, hitting him, threatening him, always shouting at him, and even forcing him to fight with other children. His experience as a child was that his older brother's loud voice was quickly followed by fists and force. He grew up to hate violence and force and had decided to always be a peaceful and gentle person. In fact, Ernesto's gentle nature was one of the things Juliana most loved about him.

Juliana was a very passionate, enthusiastic woman. When she danced, she threw herself into the music. When she laughed, she laughed long and loud. In her culture and family, people spoke loudly all the time—they laughed loudly, argued loudly, talked loudly. When they got excited, they became even noisier. It was her passion and enthusiasm that had attracted Ernesto.

So the violent fight between Juliana and Ernesto was a shock to both of them. They were horrified at what they'd done to each other, and even worse, they were afraid that their love was gone. They could not see how they could stay together after what they had done.

After meeting with their counselor, Juliana and Ernesto decided that they loved each other and wanted to try to save their relationship. Over time, the counselor helped them understand how their fight had started and why.

Their counselor asked many questions, and Ernesto and Juliana recalled the events that led to their terrible fight. Whenever they disagreed, Juliana would raise her voice, as was normal in her family. Ernesto at first tolerated this, although the loudness made it hard for him to really listen to what Juliana was saying. In the fight that finally brought them to counseling, Ernesto had been pleading with Juliana to talk more softly. And she thought she was, but what was soft for her still sounded like shouting to Ernesto. Finally, he reached out gently to put a finger to her lips to indicate that she should lower her voice.

Juliana had been beaten so often by her first husband that she thought Ernesto was going to strike her. She struck at him and shouted even louder. She saw her first husband, not Ernesto. As she screamed and struck at Ernesto, he no longer saw Juliana; he saw the brother who had bullied him. So they locked in a fight, as much with each other as with the ghosts of their separate pasts.

When they put this story together, they were able to forgive each other. But they had much work to do, because they did not understand how to communicate with each other safely. Juliana was going to have to learn to speak without raising her voice. Ernesto was going to have to understand that her louder tone was not really a threat. And Ernesto was going to have to learn how to assert himself without appearing to be a threat to Juliana. Their counselor offered them many approaches to communication that helped them slow down and fully listen to each other.

Relationships require that we learn to listen carefully and communicate in ways that our partner understands and appreciates. (We addressed ways to improve communications among couples and families in chapter 2, which you may want to review.)

### Emotional challenges

Sometimes emotional challenges are expressed through physical symptoms. They may become severe enough that we can think of them as illnesses. And sometimes physical health problems can affect our emotional health. For example, a physical disorder called "hypothyroidism" may cause a person to feel depressed. Other times, our physical symptoms result from emotional situations, such as being exposed to traumatic events.

Over many years, successful treatments have been developed to help people address their emotional symptoms. Doctors and counselors can help determine why we feel uncomfortable and help find the best way to deal with these emotional challenges.

Sometimes we experience emotional and physical symptoms in reaction to a specific issue, such as the loss of a loved one, but then after a time we feel better. However, when one or more of the symptoms persist for more than a few weeks, we need to see a health professional, such as a doctor or therapist, who can determine the appropriate way to help us.

Please note, if you or a family member are experiencing or expressing suicidal thoughts or thoughts of harming another, do not wait a few weeks; seek help immediately.

Here are some of the emotional and physical symptoms people experience:

- feeling sad, tired, empty, hopeless, or uninterested in family, friends, and favorite activities
- extreme irritability or angry outbursts
- cutting or otherwise hurting oneself intentionally
- unexplained aches, pains, headaches, cramps, or constant fatigue
- a major change in appetite, overeating or being unable to eat
- intentionally starving oneself, or intentionally overeating and then throwing up or taking laxatives
- changes in sleeping patterns, difficulty falling or staying asleep, a change in daily habits
- inability to concentrate
- worrying continuously or inability to relax, feeling on edge
- pounding or racing heart, chest pain, breathing difficulties, dizziness or unsteadiness, unexplained sweating, hot flashes or chills
- nausea, stomach discomfort
- trembling or shaking, feelings of choking
- feeling detached from oneself or reality, feeling estranged or isolated from other people
- fear in social situations that leads one to avoid most social activities
- bad dreams, flashbacks, or uncontrollable scary thoughts
- avoidance of places that remind you of a time when something bad happened
- difficulty concentrating and remembering, difficulty making decisions
- regressing, behaving like a child
- severe and sometimes rapid mood swings
- talking rapidly and jumping from one idea to another, or having racing thoughts
- frequent fidgeting
- an uncontrollable urge to repeat the same behavior
- compulsive sexual behavior, inability to stop despite wanting to

- overuse and intentional misuse of alcohol or other drugs, inability to stop using despite negative consequences

Of course, this is a long list—and we have even left many symptoms out! We have not grouped these into specific patterns because sometimes people try to diagnose themselves or a loved one. Remember: *If any of these symptoms persists for more than a few weeks, or if you feel "wrong" or "not yourself," seek help. If the actions or thoughts are suicidal, dangerous, or related to harming others, seek help immediately.*

For almost every problem you can think of, there are names and treatments. There is no need for anyone to suffer. The old belief that some people "are just crazy" is not correct. We know more now about how the brain works and how problems develop. The good news is that we have ways to treat these various situations, including counseling, medication, or both. Many people have had these problems and are now leading full, happy lives.

### Caring for your emotions

Increasing our knowledge about the causes of our emotional responses helps us improve our ability to resolve emotional challenges. Awareness is the first key to knowing that we need to tend to our emotions. Typical signs that we are out of sorts include these:

- changes in personal or household hygiene, for example, if you are normally messy but suddenly need to make everything clean and orderly, or if you are normally tidy but become sloppy
- changes in sleep patterns, needing either too much or too little
- avoidance of family or friends, or doing things to push them away
- changes in eating patterns, such as suddenly starting to overeat or being unable to eat

The signs are different for everyone. It helps to recall the last time we were unhappy or anxious, to recall any changes, and then to write down the signs. With practice, we can observe patterns about ourselves.

When we know we are out of sorts, we need to find people to talk to who can help us clarify our emotions. The support is best when it comes from people who will listen to us without judging, who we know will keep our discussions private, and who can ask us questions that help us clarify our thoughts without trying to advise us about what to do next.

Some people make a list of the other people in their lives who can help them with different kinds of problems. Maybe the people at a church group are especially good at helping sort out problems with friends or children. Perhaps a workmate knows how to listen to our relationship problems without teasing or judging us. If church is important to us, we may have church leaders or pastoral counselors who are especially good at listening. The point is to have many resources available to you—people you can talk to safely.

With a few kinds of support, though, you should be careful. Family is one. Sometimes family members are good to talk with, but we must be sure that they will listen nonjudgmentally. In some of our Latino families, there is a lot of "tough love"—family members telling each other to be strong and quit thinking about the problem. This doesn't work, because as we learned earlier with Juliana and Ernesto, emotions always find a way to get out.

Another kind of support to be careful with is a person who, instead of listening, encourages us to drink or use drugs to calm down. The companionship can feel like a kind of support, but the things we say and think under the influence of alcohol or other drugs are often confused and forgotten. Ultimately these actions make our problems worse, not better, and alcohol or drug abuse can become a problem itself.

Another way of supporting ourselves is to know which activities help us cope with strong emotions. Some people feel better after running, walking, dancing, or lifting weights. Some sing, play the guitar, write poetry, write in a diary, or listen to their favorite music. Some draw or sew. Some pray or meditate. Some cook or clean or garden. The activity doesn't matter, as long as it is safe for you and the people around you.

If reaching out to others and taking part in activities that normally soothe us does not help, then it is time to find help elsewhere. Fortunately, in many parts of the United States free or low-cost counseling services are available. Many health care plans also provide such services.

### Getting help from a counselor

Sometimes people are embarrassed to seek help from a counselor. Children use the term "*el loco*" to tease each other. Many people in relationships attack each other by saying,

"*Tú estás loco*" or "*Tú estás loca*." No one wants to be seen as crazy. So we try to push our problem aside and tough it out. But which person is wiser—the one who seeks help when he needs it, or the one who pretends there's no problem, even when that problem is making him and everyone else miserable?

Millions of people in the United States experience minor or serious emotional challenges. They seek help every day, and no one laughs at them or considers them weak. Seeing a counselor is not a sign of weakness or craziness but a sign of good sense and maturity. Emotional problems are not something to be ashamed of, and they are not something we can just "tough out." They don't go away when we ignore them.

You can find help for emotional problems from many sources:

- through a doctor or health clinic
- through a community clinic
- through your congregation
- at a community mental health center
- through a hospital
- at a university or medical school
- through a social services agency
- through your insurance provider or your employer in an "employee assistance program"

Seeing a counselor is very much like seeing a doctor. People at the counseling center will need to collect information from you and have you fill out forms. If you don't read well or understand the forms in English, you can ask for help with the forms, ask for Spanish forms, bring in someone who can help, or ask the clinic to provide a translator. These forms ask where you live, how you can be reached, whether you have insurance, and other information, which the counseling office staff can explain to you. The information is not shared with the U.S. Immigration and Customs Enforcement agency (ICE), but in some cases may be shared with your doctor or insurance provider. If you have been ordered into counseling by the court, some documentation may also need to be provided to the court, noting whether you attended the court-ordered counseling services. However, the contents of what you discuss with your counselor will remain private.

In the very first counseling session, your counselor will explain what counseling is and some of the rules of counseling. The counselor is bound by law *not* to share anything you say with another person, unless there is a reasonable suspicion of any of the following:

- that you are harming or may harm a child, elder, or vulnerable person
- that you may present a danger of violence to others
- that you are likely to harm yourself unless protective measures are taken

The law requires that the counselor must report these things, but everything else remains solely between you and your counselor. This confidentiality is very important, because it means you can talk freely with the counselor about anything that bothers you and not worry that she will tell someone else. It is so important that even if you meet your counselor by accident at a grocery store, gas station, church, or other public place, your counselor will act as though you have not met before, unless you acknowledge the counselor and greet her.

The counselor will also try to understand you and what you hope to gain from your visit. She may review your family structure and history to better understand you. That is about all that can be accomplished in the very first visit. In subsequent visits, your counselor will develop plans with you for ways to improve your life and overcome the challenges you are facing, so that you can feel happier.

Because every person is different, the ways the counselor works and the plans the counselor develops with her patients will be different from one person to the next. Counseling sessions may be offered once a week or on other schedules. The counseling work may involve additional activities on your part, such as writing in a journal, reading helpful materials, or having conversations about assigned topics with people. If your counseling involves a family member in some way, such as a child, at some point the counselor may ask you to bring in the family member. The counselor may help you practice in advance for events that may occur, so you can change your reaction to those events. She may ask many questions about your past, your family, your values, and important or tragic events that have occurred. This information helps your counselor better understand you and help you find happiness.

We Latinos are accustomed to showing great respect to professionals such as physicians and counselors. Our respect is a good thing, but sometimes it means we sit quietly and wait for the counselor to tell us what to do. Counseling does not work that way.

The counselor needs honesty from us and needs us to talk in order to help us understand what we can do to improve our well-being. Keeping silent can make the counselor's job harder. It may be helpful to think of the counselor as a teammate. You are working *together* on the same goal, which is to find a path that is conducive to you feeling better. If you are teammates, you need to talk freely. By working on the problem together, you can both succeed. This is essential to your harmony and to the well-being of the people who care about you.

---

### Suicide Prevention Help

If you are thinking about harming yourself or attempting suicide, tell someone who can help right away:

- Call your doctor's office.
- Call **911** for emergency services.
- Go to the nearest hospital emergency room.
- Call the toll-free, twenty-four-hour hotline of the National Suicide Prevention Lifeline) to be connected to a trained counselor at a suicide crisis center nearest you. In English: **1-800-273-8255** (1-800-273-TALK). In Spanish: **1-888-628-9454**

---

### Red Nacional de Prevención del Suicidio

Si usted está pensando en hacerse daño o en suicidarse, avise a alguien quien le pueda ayudar enseguida.

- Las llamadas son gratuitas desde cualquier teléfono en los Estados Unidos.
- Nuestras líneas funcionan las 24 horas todos los días de la semana, de modo que usted puede ponerse en contacto con una persona capacitada en cualquier momento en que lo necesite
- Su llamada es confidencial; esto significa que la persona que le escucha hará todo lo posible por no divulgar su identidad.
- Prestamos servicios en inglés (**1-800-273-8255**) y en español (**1-888-628-9454**).

## Summary : Chapter 3—Emotions in Harmony

Emotions are like the spices a good cook uses. So many flavors make our lives rich. When we feel unhappy, our emotions are out of harmony. There may be too much or too little spice! We feel a need to find harmony and balance. To return to that balance, we need trusted people to talk with. When those people cannot help us, when the problems persist, or when we cannot find the right people to talk with, we need to turn to a therapist or spiritual counselor. Trained professionals can help us find balance again. Like a good cook, they can help us balance the mix of flavors, so that we feel better, enjoy our lives and can be helpful, happy contributors to our families, friends, and community.

Questions to think about:

- What words do I use to describe my emotions?
- Who can I talk with about how I feel? Who will listen supportively?
- What kinds of things can I do that are healthy for my body and my emotions?

### *Reflection questions*

1. What words do I use to describe my emotions?

2. How often do I recognize my emotions?

3. Do I think some emotions are good or bad? Where or when did I learn that?

4. What could be some advantages and disadvantages of letting people know how I feel?

5. Could I learn to express all my emotions in a safe, appropriate way?

6. Have I experienced situations in my life that made me extremely afraid, or situations I wish I could forget?

7. Who can I talk with about how I feel to receive support?

8. What kinds of stress do I currently have (financial, work, marriage, medical, legal)?

9. Do I know about some common emotional illnesses that can be treated with the help of a counselor or therapist?

10. What kinds of things do I do that are healthy for my body and my emotions?

**Resumen: Capítulo 3—Emociones en armonía**

Las emociones son como los condimentos que usa un buen cocinero. Los diferentes sabores hacen más ricas nuestras vidas. Cuando nos sentimos infelices, nuestras emociones no están en armonía. ¡Hay demasiado o muy poco condimento! Sentimos la necesidad de encontrar armonía y equilibrio. Para recuperar ese equilibrio, necesitamos personas de confianza con quienes hablar. Cuando no nos pueden ayudar, cuando persisten los problemas o cuando no encontramos a la persona correcta para hablar, debemos consultar a un terapeuta o a un guía espiritual. Estos profesionales pueden ayudarnos a reencontrar nuestro equilibrio. Como en el caso de un buen cocinero, ellos nos pueden ayudar a equilibrar la mezcla de sabores, para sentirnos mejor, disfrutar nuestras vidas y ser contribuyentes útiles y felices a nuestras familias, nuestros amigos y a nuestra comunidad.

Preguntas para reflexionar:

- ¿Qué palabras uso para describir mis emociones?

- ¿Con quién puedo hablar sobre como me siento? ¿Quién me escuchará y me apoyará?

- ¿Qué tipo de cosas puedo hacer que sean sanas para mi cuerpo y mis emociones?

CHAPTER

...four...

# With My Feet on the Ground

## At a Glance

At a glance Alcohol, drugs, and tobacco need to be treated with great respect. We all know people who never use these substances and others who have made their own and others' lives miserable through use. In this chapter, you will learn about the problem of addiction and what can be done to reduce its likelihood or to treat it when it occurs. Some of the topics we cover include:

- the physical effects of alcohol and other drugs
- the physical effects of alcohol and other drugs
- what substance use, abuse, and addiction look like
- what we can do to prevent substance abuse and addiction, including *protective factors* and *risk factors*
- how to live with the chronic disease of addiction
- how the family can be involved in treatment and recovery

PEDRO IS A RECOVERING ALCOHOLIC who has been in Alcoholics Anonymous for fifteen years. He now jokes about how he tried to "quit" drinking by only using alcohol on special occasions:

> ▪▪▪ *When I drank, I got really drunk. Fortunately, I only drank at family events. You know, Sunday* fútbol *gatherings, Saturday dinners, baptisms,* quinciñeras, cumpleaños, *anniversaries, weddings, work promotions. Given the size of my family, that was pretty much three or four times a week!* ▪▪▪

In Pedro's family, as in many Latino families, a man was supposed to be able to consume a lot of alcohol and keep on going. This was a sign of his manliness. And Pedro could certainly keep up. In fact, he could consume much more than most people, and it barely seemed to affect him. The more he drank, the more he needed to consume to get drunk. But for Pedro, consuming alcohol became his life. What at first was a sign of his manliness became more important to him than his family. He spent everything on alcohol, missed work, lost jobs, and was always looking for the next party and the next drink. He may have succeeded in the "manly" art of holding his liquor, but he was failing in his duties to take care of the people around him and to be a good role model. Why? Because he had developed a disease called *alcoholism*. If he has one drink (or tries a drug), he will re-enter the horrible spiral of his disease.

Let us look at Pedro as being at one end of a long spectrum—he's at the end where someone drinks or uses drugs because his life depends on it. At the other end are people who never use at all. In between are people who have an occasional drink with no problem. And there are some people who drink to excess now and then. And at that far end, we find people like Pedro, for whom alcohol or other drugs are the center of existence.

In this chapter, you will learn about the problem of addiction, things we can do to prevent it, and how we can help people addicted to alcohol or other drugs return to healthy living. Topics include these:

- the physical effects of alcohol and other drugs
- what substance use, abuse, and addiction look like
- what we can do to prevent substance abuse and addiction, including protective factors and risk factors
- how to live with the chronic disease of addiction
- how the family can be involved in treatment and recovery

### The physical effects of alcohol and other drugs

Alcohol is the most available and commonly abused drug by people worldwide, including Latinos, so we will cover it separately.

### Alcohol

Alcohol[21] is the active chemical in wine, beer, and distilled spirits. Alcohol is a drug, just like marijuana, heroin, and many other drugs you've heard about. It is a chemical that affects the brain and body. It is important to have a basic understanding of how alcohol works in the body. From that, we can also understand how some other drugs behave.

The impact of alcohol varies from one person to another. Pedro remembers the very first time he tried alcohol: "It was special," he said. "Even now, decades later, I remember the feeling—the warmth, the sense of elation, the euphoria. From that time on, I thought about how I could have some more, and once I was old enough to get it legally, I began drinking a lot."

His cousin Felipe had his very first drink at the same time as Pedro did, but Felipe had a completely different reaction:

■■■ *I spit it out! I was embarrassed, because the other boys I was with were drinking it just fine (or pretending to), but honestly, to me it just tasted like poison. Even now, at most I can drink a beer, and I can't stand the taste of liquor. The guys make fun of me for nursing a bottle of beer the whole night and leaving half behind, but I don't care. I know who I am and what's good for my body and what isn't. I don't like the way it tastes, and it gives me a headache. I used to carry one around to be part of the group, but as I get older, I rarely even bother with that. I don't care what they think. I know who I am.* ▪▪▪

Alcohol gets into our blood with the very first sip, and we can feel its effects in about ten minutes. The alcohol we drink is absorbed through the stomach and small intestine, and then it dissolves in our blood. Our kidneys and lungs remove some of the alcohol—about 10 percent— but most of it must be processed by the liver. The liver can only process a certain amount at a time.

The concentration of alcohol in our blood is called the "blood alcohol concentration level." The higher our blood alcohol concentration, the more alcohol impairs us. This is what the police measure when they arrest an intoxicated driver and administer a Breathalyzer test or test a sample of blood. They can tell how much alcohol is in our bloodstream through these tests.

It takes the average person about one hour to process and eliminate half an ounce (fifteen milliliters) of alcohol. This is about the same amount of alcohol in a twelve-ounce can of beer. Our blood alcohol concentration increases when we drink alcohol at a rate faster than the body can process it. So if we drink several drinks in an hour, our blood alcohol concentration increases.

What happens to our brain during this time? When the alcohol reaches our brain, at first we become more self-confident and we may become talkative. Our skin may become a red color, flushing, as though we are blushing. As we consume more, our inhibitions and our judgment diminish. For example, we may say the first thing that comes to mind, even if it is embarrassing or stupid or cruel. We also get a bit clumsy.

As the level of alcohol increases, we become sleepy. We can have trouble understanding and remembering. We react slowly. We become uncoordinated and may have trouble walking straight. Our vision gets blurry. We may feel numb.

With an even higher concentration of alcohol, we get confused. We may not know where we are or what we are doing, and we may stagger about. We can get very moody, becoming aggressive, withdrawn, or affectionate. We may not feel pain as sharply as a sober person.

If we keep consuming alcohol at this pace, we will find movement difficult. We may vomit. We may lose consciousness. Eventually, the effects of alcohol put us into a coma, and we may die.

Those are the immediate effects of alcohol, the drug. With continued alcohol abuse, other health impacts include these:

- accidents due to alcohol-impaired activities, including falling or vehicle crashes
- violence due to impaired judgment
- hardening of the liver tissue, which is called cirrhosis of the liver
- stomach and intestinal ulcers
- poor nutrition
- heart damage and high blood pressure
- pancreatitis
- cancer of the mouth, esophagus, throat, liver, or breast
- weakened immune system
- fetal alcohol syndrome, which is damage to the fetus that occurs when a woman consumes alcohol while pregnant

Another effect of alcohol on the body is that, with regular use, we develop tolerance to it. The development of tolerance is one of the signs that a person may be addicted to alcohol. "Tolerance" means an increased amount of alcohol is needed to achieve the same intoxicating effect. However, the blood alcohol concentration is the same. Even though the alcohol-tolerant person does not feel the effect of the alcohol (by feeling tipsy or drunk), the person will still experience increased damage to the body. So assuming that Pedro and Felipe are both about the same size and drink three bottles of beer in an hour, they will both have the same blood alcohol concentration. Felipe, who rarely drinks, will feel sick and drunk, because his body has not developed tolerance. Pedro will barely notice, because his body has developed tolerance as a result of his regular use. However, Pedro's body will be equally damaged by the alcohol even though he doesn't feel it.

## Men and women respond differently to alcohol

Men and women process alcohol a bit differently. Women have less body water than a man of similar body weight, so if a woman and man of the same weight drink the same amount of alcohol, the woman will have a higher alcohol concentration in her blood. Menstruation also affects a woman's response to alcohol. She will have a higher blood alcohol concentration just before menstruation begins.

Generally speaking, if Maria and Mario weigh the same amount, Maria can drink about two and a half beers for every three beers that Mario drinks.

### So how much is "one drink"?

Beer, wine, and distilled spirits contain different amounts of alcohol. Within each of these categories are varying concentrations of alcohol. When we talk about one standard drink, think of the following equivalences:

- one 12-fluid-ounce **can** of beer (about 5 percent alcohol ) =
- one 8- to 9-fluid-ounce **glass** of malt liquor (about 7 percent alcohol) =
- one 5-fluid-ounce **goblet** of table wine (about 12 percent alcohol) =
- one 1.5-fluid-ounce **shot** of 80-proof spirits (such as whiskey, gin, tequila, or vodka) (about 40 percent alcohol)
- A cocktail often contains the same amount of alcohol as one to three standard drinks, depending on the type of liquor and the recipe.

### What is moderate drinking?

The amounts are different for men and women. Moderate alcohol consumption is no more than one drink per day for women and **no more than two drinks per day for men,** says the U.S. Department of Agriculture's 2010 Dietary Guidelines for Americans.

### NOT SAFE FOR PREGNANT WOMEN

Both women and men need to know that there is **no safe level of alcohol use during pregnancy!** Women who are pregnant or plan on becoming pregnant should avoid alcohol completely. Alcohol consumption may damage the baby's development.

**Other drugs**

Besides alcohol, here are some of the better-known drugs that people use and their effects:[22]

- *Nicotine.* This is the drug found in tobacco. It is both a stimulant and relaxant, and it reduces appetite. It is highly addictive.

- *Marijuana.* Marijuana comes from the cannabis plant and can be smoked, eaten, or consumed in a beverage. The drug creates euphoria, stimulates appetite, reduces inhibitions, impairs coordination, alters the sense of time, and diminishes the ability to think, learn, and remember. Long-term use can lead to addiction.

- *Stimulants.* These include cocaine, crack, caffeine (the active drug in coffee), methamphetamine, Ecstasy (MDMA), and many others. Stimulants produce feelings of alertness, euphoria, increased energy, decreased appetite, and heightened sexuality. Long-term use can lead to addiction. Overdose can lead to seizures, kidney failure, headaches, stroke, and heart attack.

- *Sedatives.* These include Valium, Librium, and sleeping pills such as Seconal. They ease anxiety, lower inhibitions, and induce sleep. Long-term use can lead to addiction. Overdose can cause death.

- *Opiates and prescription painkillers.* These include heroin, morphine, codeine, and prescription medications such as OxyContin, Fentanyl, and many others. They produce euphoria, reduce pain, and cause sedation. Long-term use can lead to addiction. Overdose can cause death.

- *Hallucinogens.* These include lysergic acid diethylamide (LSD), mescaline (peyote), psilocybin (mushrooms), and many synthetically created drugs. Hallucinogens change and distort perceptions. They can cause our senses to "cross over" so we think we are smelling a sound or hearing a color. Regular use can result in flashbacks, auditory hallucinations, and psychiatric problems.

- *Dissociative anesthetics.* These include phencyclidine (PCP or "angel dust") and ketamine. They produce visual illusions, hallucinations, feelings of strength, and personal insight. Side effects include anxiety, a sense of doom, hostile outbursts, amnesia, and paranoia. Overdose can cause death.

- *Inhalants.* These include any substances that can be sniffed to alter mood, such as gasoline, various solvents, and nitrous oxide. Inhalants are used as a cheap high to produce euphoria and altered perceptions. They make the user feel and appear dizzy and drunk. They can poison the body, cause kidney problems, liver damage, lung damage, heart issues, and death.

In addition to alcohol, nicotine, marijuana, and cocaine are the most frequently abused drugs among Latinos.[23]

---

### How much do we use?

The U.S. government collects statistics on the use of alcohol and other drugs among teens and adults in a study called the *National Survey on Drug Use and Health.* The 2010 study found these levels of use among various ethnic groups.[24]

**Percent Aged 12 or Older Who Used in the Past Month**

|  | Latino | White | African American | Asian |
|---|---|---|---|---|
| **Alcohol, binge or heavy use** | 25.1% | 24.0% | 19.8% | 12.4% |
| **Any illicit drug** | 8.1% | 9.1% | 10.7% | 3.5% |
| **Tobacco** | 21.9% | 29.5% | 27.3% | 12.5% |

---

### Use, abuse, and addiction

Throughout history, people have sought substances that change their moods. Even animals do this. Elephants, birds, and monkeys have all been known to gorge themselves on fermented fruit, seeking intoxication. In India, elephants have even been known to raid village breweries to drink alcohol! The desire to change mood seems built into us, but it must be moderated, because with mood changes come judgment errors and other problems. This is why, even before we had countries and states and laws and regulations, society had careful rituals surrounding the use of intoxicating substances. Often these substances were given a place in religious or community rituals, which helped keep their use under control.

Alcohol is only one of many kinds of mood-altering drugs. We are not accustomed to thinking of alcohol as a drug, but it is. For most of us, alcohol is simply a socially acceptable drug. But, like marijuana, heroin, methamphetamine, Valium, and many other substances, alcohol is a drug.

Many drugs were developed to serve some important medical purpose. Some drugs block pain and are essential to surgery. Some drugs induce sleep and are helpful with insomnia and other medical conditions. Some drugs reduce anxiety. Some elevate spirits and reduce depression. Some keep us awake when we need to be awake. Some increase or decrease appetite. Some, like alcohol, relax us and make us more talkative and comfortable in social settings.

Some substances have appropriate nonmedical uses. For example, alcohol is used during communion in some religious rituals. It is used to lead toasts at parties, and in moderation, to add to the enjoyment of a meal or a celebration. Some drugs, such as marijuana, salvia, and mescaline, are used in indigenous religious practices.

So we see that there are many positive uses of alcohol and other drugs. Some of these uses are medicinal and others are as part of social rituals. Unfortunately, some people are prone to misusing these substances. Some people develop a pattern of drinking or using drugs to excess. They may do this to escape from their problems, to enjoy themselves, or for other reasons. They are using the substances in ways that they were not intended to be used.

When substance use harms a person's health, relationships, or work, the person may suffer from a mild to moderate " substance use disorder," also called " substance abuse." Some of the signs that a person is abusing alcohol or another drug include these:

- failure to fulfill responsibilities at work, school, or home as a result of substance use, for example, a person who calls in sick because he is drunk or has a hangover
- using in dangerous situations, for example, using while operating heavy machinery, driving a car, taking care of children, or shingling a roof
- experiencing legal problems related to use, such as getting arrested for driving under the influence or for fighting under the influence
- continued use despite the ongoing problems caused by the substance[25]

If you remove the substance, people who have a substance abuse problem may miss the alcohol or other drug. However, they may not suffer severe consequences or strong cravings for the substance. At this point, a person is abusing the substance but has not yet become addicted to it.

Over time, a person's abuse of alcohol can turn into a severe substance use disorder, which we know as "addiction." A person can become so dependent on alcohol or another substance as to feel it is essential to life. The person will suffer physical and psychological withdrawal symptoms if the alcohol or other drug is removed. Some of these withdrawal symptoms can be quite severe and dangerous. A characteristic of this dependence is that obtaining and using the substance becomes the most important thing, even the only thing, the person thinks about. When this happens, we say the person is "addicted." Terms people use to describe this person's condition include

- "alcoholic," when a person is addicted to alcohol
- "drug addict," when a person is addicted to a drug other than alcohol
- "chemical or substance dependency," which refers to addiction to alcohol, other drugs, or both
- "substance use disorder," the psychiatric term used by the American Psychiatric Association

We will use the term "addiction" because that is what most people are familiar with.

Addiction to alcohol or to other drugs is best understood as a disease or disorder. The addiction does not occur because the person is morally weak, is a failure, is "crazy," or has some other flaw. Addiction occurs for a variety of reasons. Some people have a body chemistry that makes them more likely than other people to become addicted. Alcoholism and drug addiction can "run in families," meaning the tendency toward addiction can be passed genetically from parent to child. Other factors that contribute to a person's potential for becoming addicted are the person's experiences as a child and adolescent. Also, some substances are more addicting than others. Rather than seeing the addict as a bad person or someone we should be ashamed of, *we need to see that the person finds help.* We should not hide the person from other people.

We are still learning why some people develop an alcohol or drug addiction but others do not. We do know certain conditions make it more likely that a person will become addicted to alcohol or another drug. This is called a *predisposition* to alcoholism or other drug dependence. We also know that the younger we are when we first try alcohol or other drugs, the more likely we are to develop patterns of substance abuse or eventually addiction.

We will discuss ways to treat addiction later in this chapter. For now, let's explore some of the things we can do to prevent young people from starting down the path of substance abuse and dependence.

### Preventing substance abuse

Nicolás, his mother, and five siblings fled to the United States when Nicolás was fifteen. They came under U.S. government protection. Nicolás's father had been helping to uncover drug manufacturers in his home country and had been murdered by them; they also threatened to kill the rest of the family.

In the United States, they had established a good life, but it was hard for the children to be refugees, to have lost their father, friends, relatives, and home in just a few short weeks. The adjustment seemed to demand one thing after another from the family.

As the oldest son, Nicolás was trying to hold his family together, so he had little time to grieve the loss of his father. The new life was not easy. His mother was always sad. He felt lonely and isolated. He felt like a stranger in his new home.

Nicolás avoided drugs throughout high school, unlike some of the other teens he knew. But when he started college, a new friend offered him marijuana, and he tried it. It seemed to ease his worries a bit. Better still, he felt as though he fit in better. He had been lonely and needed friends. Marijuana helped him meet other marijuana users.

At first, he only used marijuana with his friends. Then he found ways to get some on his own, and he began smoking more. Sometimes he would use in the morning before catching the light rail to college. One time, after more than a year of this, he came out of his room and his little sister made an exaggerated sniffing noise, looked at him, and said, "Mmm, can I have some too, big brother?"

Nicolás was mortified. He hadn't known that his sister knew. He went back in his room and destroyed the pot he had. He vowed to quit then. He realized that he had started down a slippery slope. Worst of all, he felt he was setting a bad example for his younger siblings. He was failing in his duty to his family. The next time a friend offered him pot, he remembered how he had felt that morning. He remembered the look on his sister's face, and he felt terrible. He lost some of his new friends when he quit smoking pot. But that seemed a small price to pay to keep his duty to his family. And he knew he could eventually make other friends.

Nicolás's story could have been different. He might have offered his sister some marijuana. He might have tried other drugs. He might eventually have become an addict. He might have sent his family in a bad direction and created a new reason for his mother to be concerned.

Something stopped Nicolás from moving on: a *protective factor* that was embedded in his culture and upbringing. He believed strongly in values such as *familismo* and *respeto,* and in taking a leadership role in the home as the oldest male. These values rescued him. His love of family meant that he wanted to preserve his family. He did not want to see it torn apart even more by drugs. He expressed the value of *respeto* because he knew his little sister was looking up to him. He *had* to be a good role model for her. Moreover, he was disrespecting his father's memory and teachings by using drugs. Nicolás wanted to be a man who did his duty no matter how difficult. He knew that even though he would miss his marijuana friends and miss the sense of peace he found while using the drug, he had to do the right thing.

Nicolás had started on a slippery slope, and it is easy to see why. He had lost many things, including a father, in a few short years. He felt lonely and isolated. His heart was still at home even as he tried to find his way in the United States. He felt as though he could never do anything correctly, and he worried about money too. All these worries, troubles, and loneliness were *risk factors*. That is, they were like loose stones that could cause him to stumble and fall faster down the slippery slope.

So we see that Nicolás came equipped with certain factors that protected him from continuing to abuse marijuana: his values, his strong personality (learned from his father's example), his parents' teaching. And he had certain factors that put him at risk: his grief, his isolation, the heavy burdens he was carrying, and the difficulty of trying to be so mature at a young age.

We all have protective factors and risk factors, regardless of where we were born, how we got where we are, how happy or unhappy we are, what our faith is, how big or small our family is, and so forth. We might think of it as a balance scale, risk factors and protective factors setting us toward one direction or another. Risk factors increase the possibility that we will engage in alcohol or drug use or other dangerous behavior. Protective factors counteract those risks and represent the elements of our life and personality that help us make healthy choices.

Abuse of alcohol or other drugs is a real problem. We may not be able to prevent substance abuse completely, but we can reduce the prevalence of the problem by *changing the balance of the risk factors and protective factors*. This is something we can do in our families, in our congregations, at our schools, and in our communities.

Imagine two girls, neighbors, born on the same day. One is naturally strong with excellent balance. The other is naturally fast. We are not surprised when, as these girls grow older, one gets involved in gymnastics, a sport that calls for strength and balance, and the other is drawn to running, which calls for speed. Similarly, we know from scientific research that some people are born with a predisposition to addiction. It runs in families. If we are born with that predisposition, we have a slightly greater risk than someone who is born without it.

So we arrive in this world with some protective factors and some risk factors—and for some of us, the risk factors may include a predisposition toward alcoholism or other drug addiction. But we gain many other factors from our families, our communities, and society as a whole. We know that in families where the parents are more involved in their children's lives, the children are less likely to get involved in risky behavior. We also know that children are at greater risk of using alcohol and other drugs when they grow up in families where the parents frequently use alcohol or other drugs, where there is poor supervision of the children, or where there is child abuse and maltreatment.

Beyond the influence of family, local communities that feature supportive schools, after-school activities, and faith-based resources tend to protect youth from early use of alcohol and other drugs. In contrast, communities that have high poverty and violence seem to put youth at greater risk.

Finally, society as a whole also has norms and laws that influence the choices young people make. Regulations that limit access to alcohol help reduce use—for example, raising prices or taxes, reducing advertisements and discounts, or reducing the number of stores and bars. So do rules that support people and reduce racism and other forms of prejudice. Meanwhile, a lack of jobs and the presence of discrimination increase the amount of risk.[26]

The Search Institute, an organization in Minneapolis, Minnesota, has been researching protective factors in youth since the early 1990s. Researchers there have found forty developmental assets to be important in helping young people avoid risky behaviors (see appendix). These assets have been researched in the general population as well as among Latino youth and youth of color. The research shows that, on average, young people with more developmental assets engage in fewer high-risk behaviors.[27]

In our experience working with Latino families, parents, young people, and people who have substance use problems, we have observed some important aspects of Latino life that help protect our youth, as well as some aspects that put them at greater risk:

*Latino protective factors*

- connection to culture
- family unity
- support from extended family
- household responsibilities
- respect

*Connection to culture.* Connection to culture offers important benefits to young people. First, it helps them develop a sense of identity, of knowing who they are in this big world. Second, connection to a sense of history is part of our way, as humans, of feeling that we belong to something and are responsible to something bigger than ourselves. This sense helps keep us from feeling isolated. It also helps us learn and follow the expectations of our larger community. Our sense of pride in ourselves and in our culture grows from these connections. All of these attributes are strong assets for our youth.

*Family unity.* Some aspects of our strong emphasis on *familismo* can help our young people. Young people thrive when they know they are surrounded by other people who care about them, who have high expectations of them, and who are monitoring them. Our extended families really can help our Latino youth thrive. We intuitively know this, but it is rewarding to see this supported by the Search Institute's research.

*Support from extended family.* Our extended family offers many kinds of support. This support includes such concrete things as food, help finding work, help finding a place to live, and help rearing children. It also includes intangible things such as love, a sense of security, a sense of belonging, and a sense that we are needed. Having caring parents and other adults nearby is very important to our youth, and this is something that we Latinos do very well.

*Household responsibilities.* Household responsibilities are common in our families, because everyone is expected to work hard to help the family succeed. Our clear expression of these values helps set high expectations for our children and sets them on a pattern of doing well in school and in work. These responsibilities also teach children that there is a circle of care and a circle of obligation: we care for each other, but we also are expected to do our part. This increases the sense of belonging. It also keeps children involved in constructive activities, which reduces their opportunity to try risky things.

*Respect.* Our value of *respeto* can also be an important asset. *Respeto* is a two-way street: our young people are to respect their elders and follow their lead, but the elders also need to behave in ways that deserve respect. When the family and community are working well, this is the case. Young people observe older members of the family behaving positively and follow their lead. They take on their household responsibilities and follow the clear rules and expectations of the household. Again, the research shows these to be important assets that help young people avoid risky behavior. We saw in the story of Nicolás how the value of *respeto* helped pull him back from a slippery slope. He did not want to dishonor his father, and he did not want to set a bad example for his younger siblings.

### Latino risk factors
- lax attitudes toward alcohol and drug use among family and community
- certain aspects of *machismo*
- certain aspects of *fatalismo*
- stresses due to acculturation and poverty

*Lax attitudes toward alcohol and other drugs.* As Pedro observed earlier in this chapter, alcohol is a feature of family celebrations in some Latino families. Youth who see adults drink carefully and in moderation will learn to consume alcohol that way. Youth who see adults frequently drink alcohol to the point of intoxication or who see that drunkenness is tolerated or encouraged will develop an expectation that drunkenness is acceptable. They will see it as the norm.

So as parents and older members of the family, we must ask ourselves, "Which pattern are we teaching our children? Which pattern do our children observe among their friends?" If alcohol has been a frequent and overused part of family gatherings, we can arm ourselves with this new information. We can serve small amounts, use it carefully, and teach our children to respect this powerful drug. We must not think of alcohol as simply another beverage, and we must not think of intoxication as a goal. Alcohol is a powerful drug that must be treated with respect. Intoxication can put us and others at risk. A lax attitude toward easily available drugs (both legal drugs, such as painkillers, and illegal drugs, such as marijuana) can have the same effect.

*Machismo and liquor.* Although *machismo* has positive aspects, such as encouraging a man to be physically fit, work hard, and meet his obligations to the very best of his ability, one negative aspect is the belief that a true macho should be able to "hold his liquor." Young men want to prove they are worthy males. If the message they receive is that a measurement of manliness is to be able to consume a lot of liquor, then we should not be surprised when boys try to prove their worth by drinking. This expectation is foolish and must be changed. Remember the story of Felipe and Pedro? Pedro could tolerate alcohol and Felipe hated it. Who was more macho, the man whose devotion to alcohol nearly destroyed his family or the man who decided he didn't care what other people thought because he knew alcohol was bad for him. It is true that among some people, a tolerance to alcohol develops. But this tolerance is one of the aspects of addiction, and in fact, it means the alcohol is damaging them.

An alcoholic needs more alcohol to achieve the high he seeks. This means that when two beers would have once made him tipsy, his body has adjusted so that now he does not feel the impact of five beers. Unfortunately, alcohol damages the body and brain when consumed in such quantity. So what we are encouraging through this notion of "holding liquor" is that a man should become an alcoholic, lose his strength, damage his body, and weaken his brain all to prove that he is a man. It doesn't make sense. A man can't really be physically fit, work hard, and meet his obligations to the best of his ability if he is addicted to alcohol. In fact, an alcoholic's primary "duty" will eventually become finding more alcohol.

As parents and older members of the family, we need to rethink the meaning of *machismo*. The person who can "hold his liquor" is most likely far along the road to alcohol addiction. He will lose his ability to contribute to society.

Because alcoholism is a disease, people need help quitting. A false sense of machismo may prevent men from seeking help. But it takes real courage to admit you have a problem and can't quit on your own.

*Fatalismo making one passive.* Our sense that things are fated has two aspects. A positive element of *fatalismo* is that we expect "things will work out well if we do our part." This is an expression of faith in a positive future and, for those of us who are religious, in God's will. We think, "I have done my part, but I can't control the final outcome. That's in the hands of the universe (or God, or a Higher Power)."

The negative side of *fatalismo* is that some of us feel we cannot change our lives. For example, when asked in a survey, "Do you agree or disagree that it doesn't do any good to plan for the future because you don't have any control over it?" six out of ten Spanish-speaking Latinos agreed. In contrast, only three out of ten African American and fewer than two out of ten non-Latino whites agreed.[28] This tells us that many of us *feel we can't influence our future.* Yet, if we want to help our children avoid risky behaviors, we *must* change our habits to influence our future—their future. Moreover, thinking we can't influence our future flies in the face of logic. After all, many of us and our parents surmounted great difficulties *in order to change our lives.*

We have seen many families change their drinking patterns, and we have seen alcohol and drug addicts get help and quit using alcohol and drugs permanently. So we know for certain that change is possible! This negative aspect of *fatalismo*—the aspect that would lead some families to throw up their hands and say, "Well, that's just how it is" is not healthy for us or our children. It is true; we can't control the outcomes of events. But we can set events in motion using our best judgment. We have already made many changes to influence and improve our future, including seeking a better, safer place to live; learning new skills; and picking up this book and reading it.

As parents and older members of the family, we can help our young people by changing our sense of *fatalismo*. Our faith in a God or in some Higher Power does not mean we need to stand in the line of a flooding river and wait for the waves to crash over us. Rather, it calls on us to act for a positive future, trust in the best possible outcome, and then try again if that doesn't work.

*Acculturation as a stressor.* Immigration is extremely stressful. Many of us have experienced divided families, constant fears of deportation, poverty, life in troubled neighborhoods, and other issues. Our extended family helps buffer some of this; nevertheless, the pressures add up. The pressures on our children are tough too. They may have only one parent for a time, and that parent may be busy working and have less time to do things a child needs. Our children learn English faster than we do, and some of them take advantage of that to hide that they're trying risky behaviors we otherwise would forbid. And we sometimes feel "without a country." We are not really the same people we were in our home countries, and we are not really at home in the U.S. culture. This is stressful.

As parents and older members of the family, we must be honest with ourselves and our children about these stresses. Just admitting that we are stressed helps. We need to set clear limits and expectations, find time to be with and supervise our children, and find ways to be sure they are getting their physical, emotional, moral, and educational needs met.

Fortunately, many communities offer parenting workshops and other kinds of help that will enable us to cope with the stress of acculturation. Although our time is limited, even a single class can make a difference.

### What do these risk and protective factors mean for us?

As we have seen in previous chapters, many of us, especially more recent immigrants, face some very stressful situations. We may live in some pretty tough neighborhoods and have less time to be with our children than we would wish. We may have a tradition of using alcohol as a regular part of celebrations.

These are risk factors. But we've also seen that we have many strengths. These include our cultural values, our extended families, our connection to our history and culture, and our willingness to support and be involved in each other's lives.

So what do these factors mean? When we see that we are setting up risky situations, we have to change. Those of us who feel that alcohol must be a part of every event will have to change that thinking for the sake of our children. If alcohol has helped us bond with other family members, we will have to find something new. Consider Elena's story:

■■■ *My husband had been drinking more and more, and finally, he went to treatment. When he came out, my parents were mad that he had stopped drinking! He and my father had been drinking buddies. In truth, I think my father drinks too much, but that is his choice. What is not fair is that he and my mother would try to get my husband drinking again. It's not safe for him, and it is horrible for our children. I love and respect my parents, but I had to put my foot down for the sake of my husband and my children. Now at our house there is no alcohol for parties, and everyone knows it. And I have let everyone know that we may be leaving early from celebrations once the alcohol comes out. I have tried to explain. It is not easy. It has caused a rift in our family, but the lives of my husband and my children are at stake! Some members of my family stand with me, though. I can only hope that as time goes on and they see how much better my husband's and my children's lives are, they will understand. It is really hard to go against my family, but the other path would only lead us to destruction.* ■■■

Elena has made a choice to avoid a major risk factor for her and her family. She can also add to other protective factors for her children. She can be sure her children are doing important social things, such as volunteering at church and in the community. She can help them do well in school. She can be in good communication with them. Even her choice to resist the pressure of her family can be a good model for them, teaching them how to resist the pressure they will one day face from their friends who choose to try alcohol or other drugs.

Every family has risk factors and protective factors. We can think of the risk factors as weak points in a fortress, and protective factors as strong points. As busy parents and as members of the community, we can't do everything. But we can try to ensure that the weak areas are strengthened while celebrating and nourishing the strong points. For example, we may live in a troubled neighborhood. That is a weak point in the fortress. We can deal with that by supervising our children well, by getting to know our neighbors, and by finding ways to teach our children to avoid the trouble.

At the same time, we must strengthen the good things. For example, we can discover what makes our children feel competent and successful and help them grow in those things. Agustin is only ten years old, but he loves to cook, so we teach him the family recipes and help him take pride in his mastery of the craft. We make sure that he gets his homework done in time to watch his favorite cooking shows, and we introduce him to Don Tomás, who owns his own restaurant. At fourteen, Clara is fascinated by science, so we make sure she gets to the library often and takes the right classes, and we help her get into the science high school. We tell her teachers and make sure the school counselor is helping her prepare for a path to college.

These personal assets, which we help our children identify and strengthen, are their anchors. Their confidence in these assets will help them work toward a positive future and will comfort them when setbacks occur. Although strengthening our assets is not simple, this is what we can do: make sure that we are building as many of the protective factors as we can, and avoiding as many risks as we can.

### Living with addiction

As we know, some diseases need to be managed if they can't be cured. For example, Geneva developed diabetes. When she went to her doctor, she learned that to maintain her health, she would need to monitor her nutrition, check her blood sugar levels, get more exercise, and take regular medication. Adonaldo developed asthma as a young boy and, working with his doctor, he learned to follow a therapeutic regime that keeps him quite healthy. His asthma was made worse by certain pollens, so he also had to learn to use a special inhaler before the heavy pollen seasons occur.

Diabetes and asthma are two examples of *chronic disease*. A chronic disease is a long-lasting condition that can be controlled but not cured. Just like diabetes and asthma, addiction, whether it is to alcohol, marijuana, cocaine, or some other drug, can be controlled. But the person who has become an addict must change his or her life to avoid relapsing and returning to using drugs or alcohol again.

It may be difficult to think of never having a drink again, but Geneva and Adonaldo also have things they "can't" do, and they are quite happy. In fact, it is great news that someone can be treated for addiction. As with diabetes and asthma, there was a time when we had no treatment for this disease, and people simply suffered through until their last days.

When addicts quit using, we say they are "in recovery" or are "recovering alcoholics" or "recovering addicts." This indicates our understanding that they will have the condition for the rest of their lives. We understand that they will therefore need to abstain from alcohol or other mood-altering drugs, except as medically prescribed and supervised.

You will recall the story of Pedro, which opened this chapter. Here's what Pedro says today:

■ ■ ■ *I feel so bad about the suffering I put my family through. But I tell you, today, it is as though every day is a gift. I was close to losing my job. I'd been picked up for driving drunk. My kids never knew if I was going to be "good Papa" or "bad Papa." I was always selfish and wasting money on alcohol. I was mean to my wife and disrespectful to my parents. And I was getting sick all the time too! I was a shadow of my better self when I finally joined Alcoholics Anonymous. With the group's help, my Higher Power, and my family's support, I began a new life. I am grateful for every day.* ■ ■ ■

Pedro no longer drinks any alcohol, nor will he use another mood-altering drug, except when his doctor prescribes medication. His doctor knows that Pedro is addicted so he only prescribes a drug if it is absolutely needed—in which case the doctor carefully monitors Pedro's use of the prescription. Pedro and his family are happy, even though he no longer drinks at family events. As a matter of fact, after learning about Pedro's recovery, several of his relatives also joined Alcoholics Anonymous. The family may still have beer, wine, or liquor at some events, but Pedro and the other recovering family members raise a glass of iced tea. The whole family uses alcohol differently, and the children are no longer used to thinking that getting drunk is the way to celebrate.

We sometimes think that alcoholics and drug addicts are going to look like bums. They will wear tattered clothes, smell bad, and talk crazy. But the fact is that *anyone* can have an addiction: the man or woman next door, a teacher, a scientist, a priest. Anyone. Many of Pedro's friends were surprised when he went into treatment. "Sure," they said, "he got drunk, but everyone does that!" Getting drunk a lot is not normal, and making alcohol more important than family is wrong. Just like Pedro, most alcoholics look like the rest of us.

Often, the problems that the alcoholic brings into the family cause a lot of shame. The family gets used to this, so they cover up for the alcoholic. The family presents one face to the world—their "everything is fine" face—but inside the home, they never know what the addict will do next. The one place where they should feel most safe and secure is anything but that!

How did Pedro and his family go from suffering to recovery? How did they go from a place of secrets and shame to a place of happiness? If we are in this position, how can we get on the right track?

### The path to addiction

Though some addicts and alcoholics report a special feeling of attachment to drugs or alcohol with their first use, addiction doesn't always develop overnight. For many people, it takes time to develop. That's what Juan learned about his teenage children.

Juan's son Alejandro got caught with some marijuana at school. As a result, he had to see a counselor for an assessment for addiction. Juan took Alejandro to see the counselor, but Juan didn't really believe the counselor when she said Alejandro should consider treatment for addiction. "He's just hanging with the wrong crowd at school," insisted Juan. He sent his son back to school and told him to get new friends. He set up strict policies at home.

Still, two months later Juan was back at school with his son Alejandro and his daughter Rita. They'd been caught again, together. The situation had gotten worse. Now his oldest daughter was using marijuana too. "I don't understand," said Juan. "We are active in church. The kids are in soccer and folkloric dance."

Pressed for details, Juan admitted that the older kids were giving their parents a lot of "attitude," disrespecting them often. Juan, who had relied on the kids to translate school meetings, had gone to meet the principal alone, using an interpreter. That's when he learned that his son and daughter had been lying to him and his wife, and he found out just how much trouble his two oldest children had been getting into. Their grades were plummeting, they were often late or skipping school altogether, and they challenged every teacher.

That was what had brought Juan back to the counselor. He said, "My kids weren't hanging with the wrong crowd—they were the wrong crowd." Both his son and daughter went into treatment.

## Signs of addiction

The following are indicators of addiction to alcohol or another drug:

- craving, a strong desire to regularly use alcohol or other drugs
- repeatedly trying to stop and failing
- being sure to always have an adequate supply of alcohol or other drug
- spending money on the substance even though you can't afford it
- doing things to get the alcohol or other drug that you normally wouldn't, for example, lying or stealing
- feeling that you can't deal with your problems without the drug or alcohol
- doing risky things, like driving, operating machinery, or watching children while under the influence of the drug
- feeling you need to use the substance just to feel normal
- putting more and more time into getting and using drugs or alcohol

Among teens, the signs of addition include these:

- frequently missing classes or school
- sudden disinterest in school or preferred activities
- a sudden drop in grades
- health issues, such as lack of energy or lack of motivation
- decline in personal appearance and hygiene
- marked changes in behavior, such as excessive privacy, trying to hide activities from parents
- drastic changes in relationships with family or friends
- spending money, requesting money, and not showing parents what was purchased
- stealing to obtain money for drugs or alcohol
- trouble with school or other authorities for using alcohol or drugs

Some of these signs for teens may also indicate problems other than a misuse of drugs or addiction. There may be other issues, such as problems at home, or emotional problems, such as depression, adjustment challenges, learning disabilities, or anxiety. A full mental health assessment by a professional can help sort out what is actually behind these behaviors.

Alcoholics and addicts usually don't go into treatment on their own. They get there after increasing amounts of trouble. When the problem occurs with teens, as with Juan's children, troubles at school are a strong sign. With adults, the path to addiction is accompanied by relationship troubles, family troubles, job troubles, health problems, and sometimes legal problems.

### The path to recovery

We enter into recovery when we begin creating a life that does not put alcohol or other drugs at the center. We may come to this by participating in a self-help group such as Alcoholics Anonymous (AA) or Narcotics Anonymous (NA). We may also enter into recovery by attending a *treatment program*. This is a formal program that includes counseling, medical attention, and other services. Many treatment programs are out-patient programs. Patients attend these for several hours daily or for a few days a week. A benefit of outpatient treatment is that patients can continue to work and be with their families. However, in some cases, the addiction is so difficult to break that residential treatment is recommended. These programs are somewhat like a stay in a hospital, but the focus is on counseling, education, and behavior change. The residential setting can help keep patients away from the drugs they crave. Residential treatment programs can last from a few days to months.

Among adults, trying to quit and failing multiple times before entering recovery is not uncommon. That's what Bruno did.

Bruno came to treatment after attending a program for driving while intoxicated. "I had made a *promesa* to the Virgin. I pledged not to drink for two years—and I did it," he said. "I held on by my knuckles for that long, but it felt like I was in prison!" The very day his two years were up, he went out and got drunk and was arrested for driving while intoxicated. He kept drinking and finally entered a treatment program. In treatment, Bruno was able to laugh about his *promesa*. "That was not my first *promesa*, though it was my longest by far," he admitted. "I had made many others. Always I kept them, and always I celebrated by getting drunk and rewarding myself with more alcohol for days afterward. To tell you the truth, it was the thought of rewarding myself with a good long drinking binge that helped me make it two years. I think maybe after that last *promesa,* the Virgin had a better plan for me. That's why that cop was there, that's why I got arrested, and that's why I'm here in treatment!"

Bruno's treatment program, like almost all other treatment programs, emphasized the following practices:

- *Abstinence.* To enter and stay in recovery, people must abstain from all mood-altering drugs except when they are prescribed and supervised by a doctor who understands that the person has an addiction. This is true whether the person entered for alcohol, marijuana, cocaine, or some other addictive drug. Experience has shown that if we quit using alcohol but switch to marijuana, or quit cocaine but switch to alcohol, or any other combination, we will return to our addictive actions.

- *Detoxification and medical care.* Detoxification is part of the process of cleansing ourselves of the drugs we've been using. Our bodies are habituated to the chemicals we've been using, and removing them can have some dangerous side effects, depending on the drug and the severity of our addiction. Detoxification usually needs to be done under medical supervision. An addict should not try to go "cold turkey," because this can be dangerous. Medications are provided as necessary during detoxification to be sure we can regain our physical health.

- *Group and individual therapy.* During treatment, we meet with a counselor to discuss issues related to our addictive behavior. Because we have been preoccupied with alcohol and other drugs, we have denied the consequences to ourselves and to our loved ones, our employer, and the community around us. Therapy includes helping us understand the true impact of our actions on ourselves and other people. Addicts often build up a strong defense system of denial of their behavior's consequences. Therapy often involves breaking through that system, perhaps using facts gained from our family and other people we have harmed. This helps us come to grips with our behavior and motivate true change.

- *Education about addiction.* Experience has shown that most addicts and alcoholics do not really understand the medical impact of the substances they've used, their patterns of behavior, and how addiction affects other aspects of life. A portion of treatment is spent learning these important facts.

- *Unstructured fellowship with other patients.* Part of beginning recovery means learning to learn from other recovering people. Unstructured time spent getting to know other patients is often part of treatment.

- *Introduction to Alcoholics Anonymous and the Twelve Steps.* Alcoholics Anonymous (AA), Narcotics Anonymous (NA), and other mutual-help groups have proven to be invaluable for people recovering from chemical dependency. Most treatment programs incorporate the principles of AA into their routine. Most people continue attending group meetings for the rest of their lives.

- *Relapse prevention.* One hallmark of the chronic disease of addiction is that once we are addicted, we are prone to relapse—to using drugs or alcohol again. Most treatment programs help us learn techniques to avoid relapse or ways to quickly re-enter recovery when we do relapse. Regular participation in AA or NA, including following the group's programs, is one of these techniques.

- *Maintenance therapy for some addictions.* Some people may benefit from treatment with another drug, such as buprenorphine or methadone, to help live without craving and slipping back into using. This maintenance therapy may be prescribed for people who are addicted to heroin and other opium-derived drugs.

- *Treatment for other mental health issues, as needed.* In addition to chemical dependency, sometimes people have another problem, such as depression, anxiety, or post-traumatic stress disorder. It may be necessary to treat these issues separately. It is preferable if the addiction treatment program is equipped to help people with these complicated problems (called "dual disorders" or "co-occurring disorders").

### Family involvement

Addiction has been called a disease that affects the entire family. This is because the negative impact of the addicted person's behavior makes everyone else's life hard too. Imagine a family that sets off to paddle a boat down a roaring river. At first it is fun, and the family pulls together, paddling to keep the boat steady in a swift current. If one person stops paddling, the boat may go off course a little. Someone else has to paddle harder, but then that person tires more quickly. This affects someone else, who also grows weary. Eventually, everyone wears out. The boat spins aimlessly through the swift rapids, smashing against rocks. What started as a fun adventure has made everyone feel sick.

This is how addiction affects the family. Yes, it is one person's problem, but it becomes everyone's problem. This is why most treatment programs involve the family at some point. The family involvement is *not* just to learn about the alcoholic (or addict) and that person's problem. It's because we've *all* been battered by the rocks. We're all tired. We may even be angry and blame each other for the aimless battering of the boat! Family involvement helps us regain our strength as individuals and as a family. It helps us learn what it means to paddle the boat together again.

"After I had been in treatment for a while, my family began coming to family education nights," says Bruno. "At first they had an educational program for my wife and me, while the kids attended a different program. Then, after a few sessions, they started programs where all the patients and their spouse and kids dined together."

Bruno explains that at first all the kids tried to sit with all the other kids, and the parents sat with each other. After some gentle prodding by the staff, the kids began to sit with their own families and parents. "It was hard at first to know what to say to my family. I knew they were mad, and I knew I'd let them down—that I'd been letting them down for a long time, really. But we just started trying to communicate."

In separate family classes, the children were learning good communication skills that would allow them to tell Bruno and his wife what they thought and needed without being disrespectful. And in classes for the whole family, they learned how to listen to each other and avoid falling back into their usual patterns and arguments.

"After many weeks, not only our family but the other families in the room were more comfortable—you could hear a lot of chatter and laughing. We are talking more, and we are talking about fun things. I have learned about lots of things my kids are doing that I wasn't even aware of. Good things, like helping our elderly neighbors by mowing their lawns. I am so proud of them!"

After months or years of spinning about in a boat slamming against rocks, family members have learned to believe that this kind of chaos is normal. We may shout and fight, or we may withdraw and hide our feelings. It is hard to talk about our own problems and issues, and it is easier to blame someone else. By learning about how addiction has affected the entire family, though, each of us in the family can begin to take responsibility for our own problems, and we can each practice good communication. We can learn to express our feelings, such as grief, fear, shame, and anger.

Not all our problems will be solved when our loved one goes to treatment and we get some family education and learn some problem-solving skills. It is just that now we can talk about our problems honestly, and we also can learn to trust that alcohol or other drugs won't be interfering with the way we listen or talk.

## *Avoiding relapse*

One reason we call the disease of addiction a "chronic disease" is that the alcoholic or drug addict is prone to relapse. Even after years of abstinence, they can start again.

Addicts and alcoholics provide many reasons to use drugs or drink again:

- Our family wants to have alcohol at every celebration.
- The boss takes everyone out to the bar after a hard day's work.
- Friends tell me I'm "not a man" since I don't drink.
- We remember the good times we used to have when drinking.
- Our father-in-law is mad that we won't sit down and have a beer with him, and he won't accept it when we have a soda instead.
- We are worried about money and want something to calm us down.
- We have insomnia and think a little drink would help us fall asleep.
- My mother died and I am inconsolable.
- Our favorite soccer team is on television and we just want to relax.
- A friend shows up after many years and wants to get high, just like in the old days.
- A favorite song from our drinking days brings back good memories.

Look at the reasons people have started using again! How is losing one's mother anything like the hearing a favorite song? The truth is that once someone is addicted, *any* reason is good enough to start again. It is true that these cues can *trigger cravings* for alcohol or other drugs. This is why the alcoholic or drug addict needs to prepare to avoid relapse and why the family needs to be ready to help.

For social situations, some recovering alcoholics prepare responses in advance:

- "I've made a *promesa*. I can't drink."
- "I'm on probation, and I can't have a beer right now."
- "I've got an allergy and can't drink."
- "My doctor has said that this will hurt my blood pressure (or diabetes),
  so I can't drink anymore."

This kind of preparation is helpful in the early days of recovery. It can help us escape some tough social situations.

Families can help by breaking the pattern of keeping this a secret. At least within the family, we can break the stigma of addiction and quit making it a shameful thing. The family member who has made the commitment to recover from addiction should be celebrated, encouraged, and supported. This is a difficult task. Those of us who are addicts need our family's help, but we also need to stick with our recovery for the sake of our family and ourselves. They need to be able to trust us. Family is one of the best reasons to avoid relapse. We can remember that we will be letting them down if we start again.

Ultimately, honesty with everyone about our addiction or our loved one's addiction is the best thing. We are not embarrassed to tell someone we have diabetes or asthma, and we should not be embarrassed to explain that we can't drink.

In the mainstream U.S. culture, starting around 1980, there was a public movement to make it acceptable to admit that one was an alcoholic or addict and therefore could not use. At first, people tried to pressure others to drink anyway. But over time they understood. Telling alcoholics that they can have one or two drinks is like telling a diabetic that they can eat a few bowls of sugar. It's a recipe for disaster and death. As a result of public education, among many U.S. families, it is now perfectly understood that one person will drink water while someone else will have a beer. Failing to drink the same beverage has not caused these families to come apart at the seams!

This change in public attitude only happened as people told the truth about their chronic disease of addiction. Many Latino families have also made this change. We need to make sure that the truth about addiction gets out in the open, and then it will be okay for one person to have a beer while another drinks coffee or tea.

### *Alcoholics Anonymous, Narcotics Anonymous, Al-Anon*

Participating in AA or NA is one of the ways we avoid relapse, or find our way back to recovery when we do relapse. AA and NA groups are all over the world, and there are probably some near you. The meetings are held in many languages, including Spanish and Portuguese. Many people have become sober without treatment by attending AA or NA (or both). Some will go to thirty meetings in thirty days or even ninety meetings in ninety days! The members of these groups are familiar with all the lies we tell ourselves and the tricks that we pull to excuse one more drink or one last snort of cocaine.

AA, NA, and similar groups feature a program called the Twelve Steps. Following these Steps helps members become honest about their powerlessness over addiction and seek the help and wisdom they need to support recovery.

In some parts of the country, there are not enough Spanish-speaking AA groups. The solution to that is to start one. Don Antonio G., an elder in our community, has helped start many such groups. His life is a testament to the benefits of these groups, as his words show:

■■■ *I got into recovery in 1979. At that time, there were very few Spanish AA groups. After about ten years in AA, some of us started forming Spanish-speaking groups. Now we have about ten to fifteen of them.*

*Recovery is a process. It takes patience. Most alcoholics and addicts want everything "right now." Well, it doesn't work that way. It takes time to change, and you have to be honest with yourself—otherwise it won't work. But when you start changing, you become closer to your family. They want you around, when before they didn't. You stop being selfish. You spend your money with your family instead of on alcohol and drugs. You get closer to your sense of Higher Power or God.*

*AA is a discipline. You learn to understand other people, and you learn to understand yourself. When you are using, you are scared. You use a lot of energy, but you aren't going anywhere. When you stop, you start being yourself. And then you have energy to do the things that need to be done. You don't worry about problems; you think of solutions. You take care of yourself, and then you take care of your family and the people around you.*

*When you change through AA, you set an example for your family in the way you talk and in the way you are. You become a better person, and this influences the family.*

*Family members will ask, "How are you doing this?" You tell them, "AA is a place where you can change. Give it a chance. It is a slow process. It happens one day at a time. That is how it is."* ■ ■ ■

Self-help programs also exist for families. Some of these include Al-Anon, Alateen, and Nar-Anon. These groups are somewhat like AA or NA, but they are for the family members of addicts and alcoholics. All people who attend these family programs are also living with someone who has an addiction disorder, and they understand and help one another. There is no charge to participate in AA, NA, Al-Anon, Alateen, or Nar-Anon. They are run by volunteers. And no one uses their last name in these groups. They are private, confidential groups, so you can go there without fear.

To find a local AA or NA group, look in the phone book under Alcoholics Anonymous or Narcotics Anonymous. Or check online for AA at www.aa.org or for NA at www.na.org. Families can check Al-Anon at www.al-anon.alateen.org or Nar-Anon at www.nar-anon.org. All of these groups differ from each other. If you don't like one, try going a few more times. After a while, if it is still not working, try another group and stick with it for a while. It takes time to understand how these groups work and to gain their full benefit. And sometimes you feel better with one AA or NA or Al-Anon or Nar-Anon group than another.

## Summary : Chapter 4—With My Feet on the Ground

Alcohol and many other drugs have important, helpful uses. Some are part of social and religious rituals, such as alcohol used moderately as part of a celebration. Some uses are medical, such as using prescription drugs to control pain.

But we must be careful not to abuse these powerful substances.

We know that the earlier a person starts using alcohol or other drugs, the more likely serious problems will result. Fortunately, parents and community members can do many things to help reduce the risk that children or other family members will begin down this path. Our communities, our families, and the people within our families all have *risk factors* that we can guard against, as well as important *protective factors* that we can strengthen.

We can take advantage of our strong cultural roots and history to help family members see that it benefits everyone to stay healthy and avoid the risks of alcohol or other drug abuse. We can use less alcohol at family celebrations. When someone does develop the chronic disease of addiction, we can help that person get into treatment and join Alcoholics Anonymous or Narcotics Anonymous. As family members, we can learn about the disease and attend groups like Al-Anon and Nar-Anon. And when our loved one begins recovery, we can understand that the person must abstain from alcohol and other drugs, except those prescribed by a doctor. We can be honest with ourselves and with each other about the risks and extent of alcohol and other drug use, and we can take charge of improving the situation.

Questions to think about:

- What do I know about the effects of alcohol on the body?
  About the effects of other addictive drugs?

- What are my roles in and responsibilities to my family?
  How would those be affected by alcohol or drugs?

- Who do I go to for help when I notice I'm starting to drink or
  use drugs more than I want to?

*Reflection questions*

1. What do I know about the effects of alcohol in the body? About the effects of other addictive drugs?

2. How does someone become addicted—where does it start?

3. If I were addicted to alcohol or another drug, how would I know? Would I be willing to recognize my own addictive behavior?

4. Can I think of a time when I was not as responsible as I usually am, because I was drinking or using drugs?

5. How much stress do I have? Does stress, sadness, or another emotion make me think about having a drink?

6. Who can help me when life circumstances are too hard and I wish I could escape them?

7. Who do I go to for help when I notice I'm starting to drink or use more than I want to?

8. What healthy activities do I enjoy that take my mind off alcohol or drugs?

9. What are some things that make me strong as a person?

10. What is my role in and responsibility to my family? How would it be affected by alcohol or drugs?

11. Do I know about treatment programs in my community? Have I talked with someone there to find out more?

12. Does my family understand how a person with an addiction can recover?

13. Have I ever visited an Alcoholics Anonymous or Narcotics Anonymous meeting?

14. If I think I have a problem, would I ask for help from those who are already in recovery?

## Resumen: Capítulo 4—Con los pies en la tierra

El alcohol y muchas otras drogas tienen usos importantes y útiles. Algunas son parte de rituales sociales y religiosos, así como el alcohol consumido en moderación es parte de celebraciones. Algunos usos son médicos tales como medicamentos con receta para controlar el dolor.

Pero debemos tener cuidado de no consumir abusivamente de esas sustancias

Sabemos que cuando más temprano una persona comienza a consumir alcohol u otras drogas, más probable es que causen problemas serios. Afortunadamente, los padres y miembros de la comunidad pueden hacer muchas cosas para ayudar a reducir el riesgo de que los niños u otros miembros de la familia tomen ese camino. Las personas en nuestras comunidades y familias tienen todas *factores de riesgo* de los que nos podemos proteger, así como también *factores protectores* que podemos fortalecer.

Nosotros podemos aprovecharnos de nuestras raíces culturales e historias para ayudar a los familiares a darse cuenta que permanecer sanos y evitar los riesgos del consumo abusivo del alcohol y otras drogas beneficia a todos. Podemos consumir menos alcohol en las fiestas familiares. Cuando alguien desarrolla la enfermedad crónica de la adicción, podemos ayudar a esa persona a recibir tratamiento y a que asista a las reuniones de Alcohólicos Anónimos y Narcóticos Anónimos. Como familiares, podemos conocer más sobre la enfermedad y asistir a grupos como AN y NA. Y cuando nuestros seres queridos comienzan a recuperarse, podemos entender que la persona debe abstenerse de consumir alcohol y otras drogas, excepto las que el médico recete. Podemos ser sinceros con nosotros mismos y los unos a los otros sobre los riesgos y la amplitud del consumo de alcohol y otras drogas, para tomar la responsabilidad de mejorar la situación.

Preguntas para reflexionar:

- ¿Conozco de los efectos del alcohol en el cuerpo? ¿Y acerca de otras drogas adictivas?

- ¿Cuáles son los roles y responsabilidades con mi familia? ¿Cómo pueden verse afectados por el alcohol o drogas?

- ¿Dónde encuentro ayuda cuando noto que comienzo a beber o consumir drogas más de lo que deseo?

# Making a Living

## At a Glance

Making a living is very important to our mental health. On the most basic level, securing enough money affects our ability to have the food and shelter we and our loved ones need to feel safe and healthy in the world. Beyond that, making a living affects our self-esteem and other important aspects of mental well-being. Learning to navigate the economic system in the United States is no easy task, whether we have just immigrated or are from a family that has been here for generations. This chapter provides some of the most basic information a person needs to thrive in the U.S. system:

- getting an education and learning new skills
- career and job planning
- financial well-being, including budgeting and asset building

$C$ARLOTTA TELLS ABOUT her childhood between two cultures:

▪▪▪ *My mother had come up from Mexico. She was unmarried and she had no papers. I was born in the United States. My mother named me Carlotta after a cousin. She sent me back to Mexico to live with my grandparents when I was very young, so she could work and earn money. So Spanish was my first language. Then I came back, learned some English, but went back again to live with my grandparents. Each time I came back to the U.S., at least as a child, I had to relearn English. But maybe that learning and relearning helped me be a quick study later in life.* ▪▪▪

Being bilingual is just one of Carlotta's skills. Just as important are the entrepreneurial skills she learned from her grandparents. She continues her story:

▪▪▪ *My grandfather had a mango orchard, and we also raised chickens. From an early age, I learned not just to gather and prepare these things for market, but to bring them to market and to sell them. I learned to be persistent. I learned not to take no for an answer!*

*When I came back to the United States for good, I was about twelve years old. I struggled in school. But on my own, I was always fascinated by reading history, science, and stories about the natural world. I think you could call me naturally curious. Some people have even called me nosy, but it's not that. I just have this hunger to learn about everything all the time.*

*I had my own kids young in life and dropped out of high school before graduating. But I kept working, and along the way I made sure I was always learning new things and working my way up. I went from working as a basic clerk at one of those "dollar store" kind of places to being the store manager. Then I got my GED, and that enabled me to get better work. I kept my eyes open and took free courses whenever I could. Whatever course I took, whether it was two hours or two weeks, I put it on my résumé. And I'm not afraid to tell my employer I want to do more.*

*I don't like to settle for anything. I feel like I need to take what I can from each experience and then keep moving forward. And I'm not afraid to ask for what I want. I have already had people tell me "no." It's no big deal. The worst that can happen when you hear "no" is that you're just in the same place you were in before you asked. Nothing has changed. You just look for a new opportunity and ask again. You keep moving whether you hear "no" or you hear "yes." When you hear "no," you figure out a new way.* ■■■

Today Carlotta works for a large urban charity, where she helps homeless people find shelter and employment. She's seen a lot of approaches people take trying to improve their lives, and she's heard many stories. What seems to work for people is that they know their strengths, skills, attributes, and what they want.

This chapter is about *making a living*. For most of us, happiness occurs as we balance these goals:

- having adequate income to provide food, shelter, clothing, and health for ourselves and those who depend on us
- having work that we feel good about and that is connected to our values, goals, and dreams
- feeling good about ourselves as a result of achieving this balance

Not all of us want to "move up" the way Carlotta has. Some of us enjoy finding work that allows us to make enough to live and care for our family. Some of us have professional credentials and seek work similar to the work we did at home. Some of us arrive with very little or no education and may need to start with learning basic reading, writing, and math. Regardless of our background, we have many skills—we just need to learn to identify them and apply them to what's needed in the United States.

This chapter covers some of the basic skills involved in making a living in the United States:

- getting an education and learning new skills
- career and job planning
- financial well-being, including budgeting and asset building

Although this book is about Latino mental health, *financial health* is a part of mental health. It is difficult to find happiness when we struggle constantly with money or when we are doing work that makes us unhappy. This chapter helps us build a solid educational, job, and financial platform that contributes to mental health.

### Furthering our education, building our skills

Surveys of Latinos show that the majority (roughly six of every ten) of us believe that immigrants (of all types) have to speak English to "say they are a part of American Society." This view is strong regardless of income, party affiliation, fluency in English, or length of time living in the United States.

After English, Spanish is the most common language in U.S. homes. But English is still essential here, and a key to education. In fact, one of the bright points we Latinos can be quite proud of is that among recent high school graduates, more Latinos are enrolling in college than whites or African Americans. The high school dropout rate among Latinos in the United States is also falling, from close to 35 percent in 2000 to 15 percent in 2012.[29]

Clearly, many Latinos value education and value learning to speak English. Although there are communities throughout the United States where only Spanish is spoken, the moment we venture outside these communities, English is the language. For new immigrants, learning to speak, read, and write in English is essential, and many recent immigrants attend English as a second language (ESL) courses. Many elders, some of whom have lived here their entire lives and decided to learn English at last also attend these classes. We all find English helpful for a variety of reasons:

- It provides independence and a sense of pride.
- It's valuable for getting around and getting things done.
- It opens more doors to education and employment and enables us to attain higher-paying work, as well as jobs that give us more personal control over our future.
- If we have children, it enables us to communicate with their teachers, health care providers, and others.
- It improves our capacity to get news and to participate in larger community events, including those that shape the future, such as efforts toward immigration reform.

### *Learning English*

Some of us arrive in the United States from rural villages. We may have had little formal education. Others arrive with advanced degrees and years of experience working around the world. And yet we find that lack of English proficiency (or lack of personal confidence in our proficiency) places barriers in our path. Whatever our skill with "English as a second language" (ESL), we can probably find a class that suits us, and other students to learn with.

*An ESL teacher's perspective*

Janet is a volunteer teacher of ESL. About half of the students in her classes are Latino, and the rest come from around the world.

"English is the first, most important living skill, regardless of where my students come from," said Janet. "Our classes are offered at beginning, intermediate, and advanced levels. We have students who never learned to read and write in their own language, and we have students who are able to jump right in at intermediate and advanced levels. We make sure they all feel welcomed.

"At our beginning level, students learn the basics, like the letters of the alphabet, and how to read and write simple letters. But the classes are not like classes you would expect at a grammar school. They focus on learning English while learning 'living skills'—the skills you need to get around and live in the United States.

"One of my students came up from Central America. He was an excellent cook, but he was unhappy in his job. One reason was that they were treating him very unfairly, yelling at him, assigning him unpleasant and sometimes unhealthy tasks no one else had to do. He didn't know anything about the labor codes in this country. So we put a little extra time into discussing those labor codes in Spanish and English. When he saw that he really was being abused, he got sick of being bullied at his job. He quit, got another job, and was quickly promoted. Now he is the head cook in a fancy restaurant."

Janet's student benefited not only by improving his English, but by being in a friendly teaching environment that confirmed his suspicion that he was being treated unfairly at work. His improved English helped him learn about his rights and seek and succeed in his new job. According to Janet, he was bright, competitive, and had a natural sense of his rights.

"Another one of my students had never learned to read and write in her own language," Janet continued. "So we started with that—learning the alphabet. She worked hard and learned to read and write in English. We worked together for a number of years to help her gain proficiency.

"It turns out that her experience of not writing or reading had created a new skill for her. She had learned to be an excellent listener and to remember events and instructions very carefully and in the correct order the first time she heard them. She also was an excellent communicator. Rather than stumbling around when it was her time to speak, she had developed the skill of formulating her thoughts and expressing them clearly. These are rare skills in any language!

"Her lack of reading and writing were a disadvantage at first, but eventually her skills as a listener, organizer of ideas, and speaker combined with her newfound reading and writing skills. We helped her learn how to take the kinds of tests she would need to get work. Eventually, she found good work in computers, and she now also helps others learn to use computers."

*English—and other skills too*

Most ESL classes combine learning to speak, read, and write English with other living skills. For example, in one standard beginning course, students focus on developing English skills while learning these topics:

- *Personal information.* Identify personal information on forms and documents. Ask for and share these details. Ask for and give simple descriptions of family members.

- *Health.* Identify parts of the body. Identify symptoms of simple health problems. Make a doctor's appointment. Navigate a doctor's appointment.

- *Weather and clothing.* Identify seasons and types of weather. Identify basic clothing items. Discuss what clothing to wear in various kinds of weather.

- *Time and dates.* Identify and communicate times and dates. Read and comprehend calendars. Ask and answer questions about times and dates.

- *Daily actions.* Talk about daily activities. Create daily and weekly schedules. Ask and answer questions about the times and dates of activities.

- *The city.* Identify common places in the neighborhood. Identify which activities are done at common neighborhood locations. Describe neighborhoods and neighborhood locations.

- *Directions.* Discuss how to get around the city. Interpret simple city maps. Ask for and give simple directions. Identify different forms of transportation.

- *Food and restaurants.* Identify food items. Group food items based on common food groups. Discuss common eating habits and indicate food preferences. Correctly navigate ordering food in restaurants.

- *Shopping.* Identify U.S. currency. Compare prices of items. Ask salespeople questions. Understand receipts. Correctly return and exchange items.

- *Civics.* Identify the branches of U.S. government. Understand one's rights and responsibilities and how to follow the law. Understand voting and how people influence laws and regulation. Understand citizenship. Understand how to find community resources and how to become an active participant in your community.

- *Housing.* Identify various types of housing. Identify and describe rooms in a home. Read simple housing ads. Identify simple household problems. Write notes to a landlord.

- *Employment.* Identify common jobs. Match skills to jobs. Read simple job ads. Understand simple job applications and fill them out correctly.

- *On the job.* Describe past and current jobs. Read and understand work schedules and timesheets. Read and understand simple paychecks. Talk to supervisors and coworkers.

Through ESL, we also learn about nutrition, how to prepare the kinds of foods that are available in U.S. grocery stores, how to use the transportation system, how to ask for help, how to read road signs, and other basics. Intermediate and advanced classes focus on more complicated use of English while dealing with many of the same living skills.

We should not expect English proficiency to come quickly. Some studies have shown that people who have had training in their native language learn English more rapidly than those who had no such training. The pace varies from person to person and depends on age, educational background, level of literacy in native language, and opportunities to interact with native English speakers. In general, a person who knows no English will require five to seven years to be able to perform most communication tasks, including academic ones. Some research indicates that it requires 500 to 1,000 hours for an adult who is literate in his native language to be able to communicate in a second language well enough to satisfy basic needs, work, and have limited social interactions.[30]

---

**Finding ESL classes**

Free classes in English as a second language (ESL) can be found by checking various resources:

- local school districts; many offer ESL, or know where classes are held
- workforce and resource centers set up by nonprofit groups
- community colleges
- other members of your language community who have been in the United States longer
- on the internet by searching terms like "ESL" and "English as second language," and including the name of your city or state
- if available, the literacy council in the state where you live

Some sites listed on the internet state they offer assistance learning English, and there are fee-based programs as well.

---

*Improving conversational skills*

A variety of personal and outside barriers can keep us from becoming proficient in English:

- feeling isolated, or keeping oneself isolated
- fear of being incorrect or publicly embarrassed
- discomfort at having an accent
- fear or frustration with being misunderstood
- feelings of inferiority
- fear that we are too old to learn something new

When we first arrive, we can feel very isolated, confused, and alone. Over time, we gain comfort and learn how to get around, but we can still feel isolated, especially if we are not learning English. Many of us feel we are the only ones going through this.

ESL courses help us overcome the sense that we are alone in our struggles. It helps to know that others are struggling with the same issues. We can learn how they handle the struggle, which makes our own learning easier.

Our fears can keep us isolated and prevent us from learning new things. Researchers at Purdue University studied both Mexican and Chinese immigrants who lived in "ethnic enclaves" in the United States. These are communities where people speak only their native language. For the most part, they buy the things they need and even find work without having to leave the area. The researchers found that people in those communities were less likely to learn or become fluent in English.[31] This makes sense. Getting out among English speakers pushes us to learn English: that's what Marta discovered.

### Marta's story: Speak out!

Marta had been a good student in Mexico City, where she had finished high school. Her husband had had several years of college there. When they moved to the United States, they settled in a Spanish-speaking community in a large Midwestern city. Her husband found work right away, and she was able to stay home and care for the children. The children became excellent students and spoke English well. They had many friends, both Spanish-speaking and English-speaking.

Marta was able to get almost everything she needed for the family in her neighborhood, and she had some good friends there. But as time went on, she began to feel left behind. Her husband had all his work friends, and his English kept improving. When his work friends came to visit, she sometimes felt left out, since they often spoke English to make the English-only speakers feel welcomed. Half of her children's playmates only spoke English, and Marta could barely communicate with their mothers and fathers. Her frustration and embarrassment grew. Finally, she enrolled in ESL courses at the community center.

Her teacher praised her often. Sometimes she would try her English at home, but the children giggled and she felt embarrassed. She kept going to school and the teachers kept moving her up in her ESL classes. One day her teacher came to her and said, "Marta, you know so much, yet I hear from you that you are afraid to speak even at home. And you don't often speak English even in class. I've seen all your test scores. I know you understand everything. We need to get you speaking English. That's just how it is."

The next week, the ESL class took a field trip to a Vietnamese restaurant halfway across town. Their instructor told them they had to order in English. People giggled and ordered. When it was Marta's turn, she ordered a Vietnamese food even her teacher couldn't pronounce, but she struggled through it, and the waiter understood. Then she tried a few more sentences on the waiter, asking about how the food was made and what was in it.

Marta was excited when she talked to her teacher the next week. "That was the first time I'd used English with someone outside my home. They understood me!"

"All it takes is a little courage," said her teacher. "You spoke very well."

Marta kept up with her classes. Her children entered high school, and she found work during the day in a restaurant. She started in the kitchen, and when she was ready, moved out to serve people—speaking English or Spanish, as the customer needed.

As Marta discovered, the only way to succeed with English (or any other second language) is to make mistakes. English is not an easy language. Even native English speakers get confused by their own grammar, and the spelling of words is often ridiculous. In what other language would "rein," "rain," and "reign" all sound exactly alike yet be spelled differently and have completely different meanings?

### Other educational opportunities

The United States offers many options for education. For those of us who dropped out of high school here, or did not have that option in our home regions, we can take preparation courses to complete the GED (General Educational Development) test. This test is very important for a job search, because a high school diploma or GED equivalency is required by many employers.

Computer literacy is also essential for many jobs. Many job applications are now taken only online, via the computer. Along with GED courses, many local organizations offer classes in basic computer skills at low cost.

Courses in most school districts can help you with this. Other courses can be found at community colleges, vocational and technical schools, colleges, and universities. There are also relatively brief classes to help you learn skills in customer service. There are even free online college courses (although these do not give college credit).

Employers also offer training in a variety of topics. Even if the training is only for a few hours or one day, it is important to record the training for our resumes. For example, in a warehouse, we may receive training in how to operate a forklift, how to lift heavy items, and so forth. In an assembly job, we may receive training in quality assurance and control. In a retail job, we may receive training in customer satisfaction, handling complaints, and so forth. In a flooring company, we may be sent to school to learn how to install carpet and vinyl. In an office job, we may be offered training to learn new computer software. In an administrative job, we may learn about the rules regarding how to treat confidential information. Each of these experiences represents an educational accomplishment on our part. They matter to us—and they matter to employers. They should go on our resumes and be presented to our next potential employers. The presence of a skill on a resume can help a potential employer decide to hire us.

### Job and career planning

For those of us who come from urban areas or have professional skills and training, finding work in the United States is not unlike finding work at home. It requires a mix of networking with others in the profession, sending out resumes, going on informational interviews, and making sure our resume shows us in the best light.

For those of us who came from smaller towns or with less education, finding work is very different in the United States. At home, we often got work through other family members, friends, or others in town who knew us. The personal touch mattered. The process in the United States is quite different and much less personal, although personal skills still matter.

Some of us came from settings where poverty was the norm, and our focus was very much on surviving rather than trying to develop some kind of career or job path. We may need to start with this same approach in the United States. But if we wish to have a more comfortable life, we will need to develop a mix of skills that is valuable to employers or else set out on our own to operate our own businesses.

The best thing we can do in our job search is to seek help through a community agency, workforce development office, books, and other resources. These four steps serve as a basic outline for the process, but these can be refined as we proceed with assistance from one of these services.

1. ASSESS YOURSELF

    a. Understand your values. Because much of our lives are spent working, we need to be sure the work we do aligns with our values.

    b. Understand what we want from a job. Some of us want to make enough to live on and support our families. Others of us seek certain hours or flexibility. Others seek various challenges. What we need from a job influences the kinds of jobs we might seek.

    c. Understand and list your educational background, skills, knowledge, and personal attributes. These need to match up with the kinds of jobs we might do. We are more likely to succeed in work in which we have had some previous success or in which our existing skills can transfer to the new work while we build additional abilities.

    d. Understand the basic "soft skills" for working in the United States, including how to interview, how to dress for an interview, what employers expect in terms of timeliness and productivity, and similar qualities.

    Asking these questions can help you with your self-assessment:

    • What are my personal values, the principles that guide my life? What are my responsibilities toward my family? Toward my community? Toward society?

    • What are my skills? Do I need to use the computer to search for jobs, write an application, and create a resume? To practice my English? To communicate with my family in my home country, or to do research (to find out information)?

    • How do I prepare for an interview? What do I need to wear? What should I say?

    • What is appropriate behavior at work? Why is it important that I always arrive to work on time? Should I always look my best when I go to work? Why is it important?

2. EXPLORE AND CONSIDER OPTIONS

    a. Find out what kinds of jobs use the skills you have and meet your requirements.

    b. Talk to people who have those jobs to find out what the work is like. Ask them for suggestions on how to find similar work.

    c. Talk to employers to learn about the jobs they have and the skills that match them.

d. Connect with a local workforce center, community service agency, or other group that can assist with job seeking.

Asking these questions can help you explore options:

- If I say, "I just want to get a job," is that enough? Or should I consider a career? A profession? How?

- What paperwork do I need to work in this country? What sorts of certification or diplomas are needed to pursue the kind of work I would like to do? Do I have these? If not, what do I need to do to obtain them?

- How might my current skills and experiences transfer to another line of work? What professions or technical careers exist for a person like me?

- How do I get to know my neighbors? How do I build a network of people? How do I find employers in the line of work I wish to pursue?

3. SET GOALS

a. Understand the nature of goals. Good goals are SMART:

**S**pecific

**M**easurable

Achievable

**R**ealistic

Timely

For example, the goal "Find a job" is not a SMART goal, because it is not specific and does not include a timeline. Contrast this with "Interview five possible construction employers within the next four weeks." This is a specific goal, it can be measured (you either interviewed with five or you didn't), it is achievable (if five such employers work in the area), it is realistic, and it is timely (with a deadline of four weeks).

b. Keep several options in mind. For example, a person who has not settled on a specific job might explore jobs in construction, painting, cooking, and health services. As she explores these options, her goal will become more specific.

Asking these questions can help you set goals:

- How do I use my skills and my past experience to set up my goals? To figure out what career I should get into?

- What steps should I follow to gain the work I want?

- Are my goals realistic? How much time will it take me to achieve them?

4. DEVELOP A PLAN AND GO TO WORK ON IT

   a. Determine whether you need additional skills, experience, education, or information—and if so, how to develop these.

   b. Determine how to use your current network of contacts and to expand it as needed. This network includes potential employers, friends, family, professional contacts, contacts through church or community participation—anyone who may know about job opportunities.

   c. Understand how to expand on your current skills, such as through volunteering or accepting work that will lead to skill improvement.

   d. Find a support network of friends or peers who can help you keep on track with your goals, find opportunities, and whom you can also help.

   e. Review and adjust the plan as you learn more about the work you are pursuing.

Asking these questions can help you pursue your plan:

- Who can help me achieve my plan? Where can I find the support I need?

- Am I meeting the goals I set? Or do I need to adjust my goals? What should I add, remove, or change?

### Transferring skills and education

Those of us who arrive here with advanced education may find that work in our fields is hard to come by. Degrees may not be accepted. Re-education may be an option when the resources are available. Using networks to find our way to an employer who accepts our experience is another option. However, it often becomes necessary to retrain. Let's look at two people who did that. First, meet Josefina.

Josefina had recently moved to the United States from Venezuela, where she had extensive experience as an engineer, including internationally. But she learned that the systems she was familiar with were not used in the same way in her new country. In addition, for personal reasons, she was uncomfortable contributing her talents to the few U.S. corporations that could use her specialty. But most important to her was that she was a single mother with a daughter who had just turned sixteen. She wanted to focus the next three years of her life on helping her daughter finish high school and get into a good college. So Josefina wants to transfer her skills and experience into part-time work that will let her help her daughter in this important transition. She is working with a job coach from a local community assistance agency to determine new jobs she might undertake. She is interested in shifting her experience to the medical field. While seeking work, she has volunteered at the local Red Cross, where she has earned a certificate in cardiopulmonary resuscitation (CPR). She is considering training as an emergency medical technician (EMT).

Now, meet Arnoldo. Like Josefina, Arnoldo was an engineer. He had been in the United States for two years and had applied for engineering jobs all over the country, with no success. Part of this was due to an economic downturn, and part was due to his lack of familiarity with U.S. engineering expectations. But he had a good mix of skills. In his position as an engineer, he had often been the man to talk to clients and customers. He was also familiar with assessing the risk involved when comparing alternate engineering solutions to problems. He transferred his customer-service skills and understanding of risk to become an insurance broker in his new country. He set up his own agency as part of a large insurance company, which helped him get licensure. His bilingual skills meant he could serve Spanish-speaking clients while communicating in English with the insurance company. He is making enough income selling insurance. Still, he misses his engineering work, and so has found some U.S. mentors to help him understand what kind of retraining he needs to complete to return to work as an engineer.

Josefina and Arnoldo both arrived in the United States with advanced training in similar fields and with years of experience, but for very different reasons they were not working in their fields of choice. Changing fields is not uncommon for people in the United States, whether they are Latino or not. Paths are seldom straightforward, and we must knock on many doors to find out which will open.

Some of us arrive with little education. Some of us may lack documentation. There are still ways to work and earn a living here, and ways to transfer skills. Experiences in farm labor, working with animals, cooking, or selling items at a market all require skills that can transfer to a line of work in the United States. Community service agencies can help determine which skills will transfer and what kinds of positions are open.

### Starting a new business

Rather than finding employment with a company, some people choose to start their own businesses. That's what Guillermo did.

Now thirty-two, Guillermo had grown up in a village in Peru where he had gone to work after sixth grade. He arrived in the United States at the age of twenty-two and began learning English. Later he picked up math, writing, and other skills. He had been working hard for most of his life and took pride in his ability to stick with a tough job until it was done.

Most recently, he had been working for a carpet-cleaning company. He enjoyed the work, especially seeing how the carpets looked when he was finished. His boss always paid in cash. But Guillermo became increasingly dissatisfied with the owner of the company. He observed that the boss did not show a good work ethic. Sometimes the boss ignored customer complaints about other workers, sent Guillermo back to fix their mistakes, but did not reprimand or fire the sloppy employees. The boss didn't seem to care whether his workers showed up on time. Guillermo wanted to be part of a company that took pride in good work. He decided he wanted to start his own cleaning company.

Guillermo was an undocumented worker, but he was able to obtain an Individual Tax Identification Number (ITIN) that would allow him to use the U.S. banking system, pay taxes, and get a microloan. With the loan and his own cash, he purchased enough equipment to get started. Within weeks he was working full-time and making good money.

One of his clients was so pleased with Guillermo's work at her home that she referred him to a restaurant franchise where she was vice president. Her company asked him to submit a proposal to clean all the franchise's restaurants in the state on a regular schedule. Guillermo had never developed a proposal, but with the help of a job coach, he researched on the Internet how to write and submit one, how to price the work, and other details. He developed a complete plan, submitted it, and won the bid. Business is now so brisk that he has hired a cousin full-time and sometimes needs to bring in extra help.

Guillermo's skills, work ethic, and resourcefulness helped him get his business under way. Having a good work ethic and the capacity to seek help are important assets. These assets will serve us regardless of the kind of work we pursue.

### Overcoming barriers

We face a number of issues when seeking work. Among those most frequently mentioned are child care, English language skills, computer skills and access, fear of loss, immigration status, and lack of understanding of workers' rights.

### Child care

In the United States, many households rely on two incomes to make enough money to live on. In a two-parent family, both parents may work, one parent may work full-time while the other works part-time, one parent may work two jobs, or some other combination. When both parents are working, child care can be a challenge. It is not safe to leave young children home alone. When we have papers, we can apply for child-care assistance through government agencies. If we are paying taxes, we may get credits toward child care. Many families rely on family members, neighbors, friends from church or others to help out. Some groups of families form child-care or babysitting pools in which they alternate taking care of each other's children. Others may find ways to work at home while the children are home. So long as any care providers are trustworthy and the children are safe, all these options can help us find work.

### English language skills

As we noted earlier, inability to speak English is a major barrier. Ability to speak English may also be hampered when one's accent interferes with an English speaker's ability to understand.

Lorenzo finds himself up against this barrier. He has mastered every task in the warehouse—stocking, operating the forklift, handling inventory. He is ready to move up, and his supervisor has talked to him about taking a shift leader position. But Lorenzo is concerned. His current supervisor understands Lorenzo's English very well, but Lorenzo has observed that in other situations, English speakers don't always understand him. They may ask him to repeat himself, which embarrasses him. If he becomes a shift leader, he'll have to attend meetings and speak with the manager, who seems to have trouble understanding him. Lorenzo isn't sure whether to stick with a safe bet or take the new job.

*Computer skills and access*

Applying for many jobs in the United States occurs on a computer. If we don't own a computer, we can use computers that are available at libraries and other sites. If we lack computer skills, many agencies teach these. For example, local school districts often offer enrichment courses.

*Fear of loss*

When we have had many difficulties and losses, we tend to hold more dearly to the things we have. In some cases, people may be offered promotions but choose to stay with the job position that they have because they feel the promotion puts them at greater risk. Let's consider this situation involving several factory workers.

Ernest, the owner of a food-packaging factory, called in his friend Rosamaria to talk to three of his employees. The three had been good, solid workers, helping to train many other workers, and Ernest had offered to promote them several times. Each time they turned him down. He was confused—why wouldn't they want to become shift supervisors, earn more money, and be able to set schedules? Rosamaria had placed many fine workers at his factory, including these three, so he thought she could help.

Rosamaria soon discovered that the employees really didn't even want to talk with her much. They were upset and worried that they had been pulled off the factory line for a meeting! After some questions, she learned that they were comfortable with what they were doing and enjoyed it. Each one worried that a promotion would mean greater risk: they thought if they made a mistake, they would be more exposed, and the owner would fire them. For these three, it was enough to do excellent work, make the money they were making, and be appreciated by Ernest.

Decisions about promotions need to be weighed carefully. Often we can gain much through promotion—not only more money, but also greater control of our schedules and our future, as well as access to more promotions. But this access does require the willingness to take a risk.

*Immigration status*

Those of us in the United States without documentation face many hurdles. Our personal networks can help us find employers who do not verify documentation or who pay cash. However, we still need to pay taxes on work done here, and we may wish to use the

U.S. banking system. We can obtain an ITIN, which will also allow us to apply for a tax refund at the year's end. Should comprehensive immigration reform be passed in the United States, most proposals include a way for some undocumented people to apply for conditional legal status. Proof that one has been paying taxes or will pay due taxes may become a part of that process.

### *Lack of understanding of workers' rights*

In the United States, workers have rights, regardless of their immigration status. Unfortunately, for fear of being fired, some people will tolerate abusive employment practices. If a person thinks his rights have been violated, he can report the employer to a government enforcement agency and may be able to bring a lawsuit to recover losses. Here is a general summary of basic workers' rights:[32]

1. You have the right not to be retaliated against. Your employer can't try to punish you, for example, by threatening to report you to immigration or the police if you try to enforce your rights.

2. You have the right to be paid for all the work you do. The U.S. federal and state governments have minimum wage rules (which vary by state). Your employer is obligated to pay this minimum (although your employment contract may state a higher amount). Overtime pay is at one-and-a-half times the regular wage for time over forty hours per week.

3. You have the right not to be discriminated against. You cannot be treated differently or badly at work because of your gender, race, national origin, color, religion, or disability.

4. Female workers may not be treated differently based on sex or pregnancy. This is discrimination. No worker, male or female, can be sexually harassed, made to perform sexual acts or favors, or subjected to sexually offensive comments.

5. You have the right to a healthy, safe workplace. Housing, bathrooms, and drinking water must all be clean, safe, and accessible. You may seek medical treatment if you are injured or get sick while at work. If you work with pesticides or dangerous chemicals, you have the right to wash your hands in clean water after using the chemicals. Your employer must provide training during the first five days of work

Your employer must tell you where and when pesticides were used, so you can avoid exposure. If the chemicals require protective equipment, your employer must provide equipment in clean, good condition.

6. You have the right to join a union and bargain collectively. With few exceptions, all workers in the United States have the right to form and join a union, regardless of their immigration status. Your employer cannot take action against you for doing so. You can join with other workers to improve wages and working conditions; attend public speeches, rallies, and demonstrations; and join a union or other worker organization.

7. You have the right to other protections in the state where you work.

8. You have the right to leave an abusive employment situation. You don't have to stay in your job if your employer is abusing you. However, if you came to the United States on an employment-based visa and you leave your employer, your visa status will no longer be valid. Depending on the type of visa you have, you may be able to change visa categories or employers. You may be able to remain in the United States legally to pursue a legal claim. You may also make a formal complaint or file a lawsuit against your employer while you are still working.

---

### Workers' rights

If you are mistreated or your rights are violated, call the **National Human Trafficking Resource Center** on its 24-hour toll-free hotline, **1-888-373-7888** (a non-governmental organization). Or call the **Worker Exploitation Task Force Complaint Line** run by the U.S. Department of Justice at **1-888-428-7581.**

There are severe penalties for an employer who tries to punish workers because they pursue their rights. If you are experiencing problems with your current employer, contact these hotlines. The person answering the phone will be able to connect you with a local organization that can speak with you about your options.

## *Pride in our work*

Most of us take great pride in our work. We are satisfied by a job done well and by our contributions to the support and well-being of our families. Beyond its role in our survival, work is important to our sense of identity and sense of contribution to others. This is true for the person whose job is to take care of the household, and it is true for the person who earns wages.

Many of us have left difficult situations in our home country only to find new difficult situations in the United States. We may lose track of the fact that we should feel proud of ourselves and our accomplishments, as well as those of our family members, whom we have supported in as many ways as possible.

That was true for a young man named Simon. When his English teacher, Laura, said "It's time to write a resume," he threw his hands in the air.

"We don't need to learn this," he said. "We would never aspire to this. We won't have a chance at a job that requires a resume."

Laura said, "Write one; you may have a need for it."

Simon wanted to start his own construction business, but he knew he needed more experience in the United States before he could do that. He had worked on many houses in his home country. But he had been frustrated finding work since moving here.

"Simon, you can't give up," said Laura. "You need to keep applying. When you tell me that, it's like you are saying 'I'm not good enough to need a resume.' You must say to yourself, *'Sí, se puede*. Yes I can.' I am confident you will find work. The economy is slow right now, and people aren't building houses. When the market speeds up, though, they will need people with your skills. And you'll need that resume."

We can feel worn down by the frustrations of feeling part of one country and part of a new one, the difficulties navigating through the U.S. systems, and the difficulty of getting work that matches our dreams and skills. But time and again, we Latinos have proven ourselves up to the challenge. We look around and see others who came to the United States many generations before us, as well as more recent arrivals, who are happily employed. Pride in ourselves, in our skills, and in our families can carry us through difficult times.

### Managing our money

It has been said that money can't buy happiness—but it will give you a chance to bid on it!

More seriously, we all know that lack of sufficient money to pay for our basic needs, as well as help us with a few luxuries for our family, can contribute to personal and familial strife and unhappiness. Couples often fight about money. Learning to manage money in the United States requires that we understand the nation's basic financial system.

Most of us arrive in the United States with good knowledge of how to manage our money in our own country. But the system here is quite different. Some of us came from countries where the banking and financial system was very unstable and perhaps not to be trusted. Some of us came from rural areas where banks were rarely available. And some of us were accustomed to keeping our wealth in land, in cattle, in crops, or in other items. This means that many of us arrive in the United States thinking in terms of hard cash. We may store our money in hiding places, and we don't understand the advantages and risks of using loans and other forms of credit, such as credit cards. Those of us who are without documents may also live with the false idea that we cannot use the U.S. banking system. In fact, we can do so safely. That's what Beatriz discovered.

### Beatriz's story

Beatriz had been making just enough money in her job cleaning hotel rooms. The cash tips that customers left certainly helped, but when she got her check every other week, she had to take it to a Spanish-speaking check-cashing service. The service was charging a fee to cash her checks. In a typical pay period, she made about $600 after taxes and other deductions. She would go to cash the check and get only $580! She began to add it up and realized that in a year she was paying more than $500 to the check-cashing service—just so she could get the money that she had earned through her hard work. It was even worse when she brought a personal check to the check-cashing service and learned the service intended to take almost one-third of the amount as a fee.

That $500 out of her pocket made her mad, but it wasn't until she enrolled in a financial class for immigrant workers that she found out she could be saving that money. They helped her understand how to get an ITIN so she could use the banking system. (ITIN stands for "Individual Tax Identification Number.")

"That will save you $500 during the year, but you'll do even better when you get your tax refund," the instructor told Beatriz.

"Tax refund? Won't I get in trouble if I do that?" asked Beatriz, who did not have papers.

Her instructor explained that the U.S. department that dealt with taxes, the Internal Revenue Service (IRS), did not give information to the department that dealt with undocumented workers (the USCIS). "With an ITIN, you can use the banks, deposit your checks, save money in a safe place, and file for any tax refund you may be due at the end of the year." The instructor also explained that during March, the organization offered free tax preparation services and would help Beatriz file her first tax return. The instructor said if Beatriz filed a return, it was likely that, because of her income level, she would get a tax refund.

It turned out that the bank in her neighborhood was accustomed to doing business with Spanish-speaking customers and even had a bank teller who spoke Spanish.

Although the U.S. financial system is by no means perfect, it is safe, and money placed in a bank or credit union is insured up to $250,000. That means if something happened to the bank, your money is still safe. Understanding how to use the financial system can help us take advantage of some of its better features, earn interest on our savings, and build a credit record that allows us to borrow money for large purchases, such as homes and automobiles. Lack of understanding can cost us dearly, as Beatriz discovered.

Beatriz was fortunate to find a community service agency that offered financial counseling. Many organizations offer such services. Spanish-only speakers may begin a search for similar programs by contacting a local nonprofit group that serves Spanish speakers. They may be able to help locate classes in Spanish. Classes in English are often offered through local school districts or other sources.

### Financial skills for all of us
Like Beatriz, we can all expand our financial skills. With these skills, we better understand how money works in the world: how someone earns it, manages it, invests it (to help it grow), and even donates it to help others. And we can make informed, effective decisions with all of our financial resources.

Try these seven steps to expand your own financial skills:

1. Understand your values and set financial goals, including savings goals.

2. Develop a budget.

3. Understand credit.

4. Pay taxes and use the tax system.

5. Use the banking system.

6. Understand the costs of ownership (for example, when deciding to buy a vehicle).

7. Begin to build assets.

An overview of these steps follows. It's important to seek guidance and classes to understand these issues. By following these steps, we can gain better financial understanding. This can help us achieve important goals and dreams, such as educating our families, owning a home, or starting our own business.

*Step 1: Understand your values and set financial goals, including savings goals.*
Our personal values and our family history with money help shape how we use money. If we grew up in poverty, we may not be familiar with some ways people save money and "grow" it to a larger amount through investments. If we grew up in a family where one person managed all the money, we may never have learned how to manage it ourselves. If we grew up in a region with very set economic classes, we may have been conditioned to expect that if we were wealthy, we would always have enough, and if we were not wealthy, we had to be satisfied with what we had. These values, whatever they were, shape how we think of money and use it.

One of the first things we have to learn to do is to *pay ourselves first*. We may be used to paying all our bills, buying the groceries, and paying for other necessities, and then, if there is something left over, we save it. This is the reverse of how things should be. We need to set a budget (see step 2), and part of that budget involves saving money for ourselves and our future first. Here are some ways that people do this:

- At the end of the day, save your coins in a jar. Beatriz puts half the tip money she gets each day in a jar. She takes this to the bank every week and deposits it into an interest-paying account. This means she is saving roughly $20 to $40 a week from tips (which equals at least $80 per month).

- When a loan or credit card is paid off, keep paying that same amount to yourself. Beatriz had taken a small credit card loan to buy a vacuum cleaner for her apartment. She pays $32 each month. In two more months, she will pay off the loan. After that, she plans to put the $32 each month into her savings.

- Save 5 to 10 percent from your paycheck in a savings account. Beatriz does not have a large paycheck. She is working to put 3 percent of each paycheck into savings, which will be about $18 per paycheck (which equals $36 per month).

- Save some of the extra money (tax refunds, gifts) that you might receive. Beatriz does not get extra money, but she is hoping to receive a refund when she files her taxes. She plans to save at least half of that. Now let's look at the totals. Without the tax refund, Beatriz will soon be saving $148 each month, or $1,776 per year. If she gets a tax refund and saves it, her savings account may show even more money!

If we want to save more money than we are currently saving, there are only two ways to do that:

1. increase income
2. reduce spending

We can increase income by getting a better-paying job, taking a second job, or finding ways to invest our money so that it brings in more income (called "unearned income"). We can reduce spending by taking a careful look at our spending habits, which happens as we develop a budget (see step 2).

But there are many ways to save money that we may not think about. For example, if we are accustomed to buying a $2 cup of coffee on the way to work five days a week, we can save about $40 each month by breaking our coffee habit. Or consider the construction worker who stops for a $5 fast-food lunch every workday. In a year, he has spent $1,300 on lunches. Over twenty years, he or she will spend at least $26,000. Bringing lunch seems like a pretty good idea when viewed that way. (Similarly, think about what a daily pack of cigarettes costs over the long term.)

An important way to manage expenses is to separate "needs" from "wants." A "need" is something that is essential to our present survival and future well-being. Everything else is a "want"—something extra. It is easy to get these confused: everyone else has a car, so don't we need one too? The difference between needs and wants is important, because we must make enough money to cover our needs, but everything after that can be saved instead of spent. Consider the following comparisons:

- We need a place to live. Usually that means we have to pay rent or a mortgage. But we don't need to live in the fancy place with a swimming pool.

- We need neatly trimmed nails for our work. But we want a professional manicure. We can cut our own nails.

- We need some form of leisure activity to relax our brains. But we want cable television so we can sit and watch our favorite sports shows. We could instead go for a walk, use the library, or visit a friend.

- We need retirement savings to insure our future well-being. But we want to spend money on a boat.

Earlier in this chapter we learned about SMART goals: specific, measurable, achievable, realistic, and time-specific. This approach also applies when figuring out ways to save money or increase income. Whatever goals we set to save or earn more money, they must be specific, measurable, achievable, realistic, and time-specific. For example, if Beatriz had said, "I will save enough money to buy a house," she would not be making a SMART goal. Instead, she could say, "I will save $10,000 in six years to use as a down payment for a house. I will do this by putting away $148 each month every year in a savings account that I will not withdraw money from." That's a smart goal: it is a specific amount of money, and based on her current, realistic plan, Beatriz should actually be able to save $10,656 in six years.

*Step 2: Develop a budget*
A budget is a detailed plan for how we will manage income and plan for expenses. It's a very powerful tool, because it lets us see how we are using our income and to imagine

ways to do more with the same amount. It helps us plan for both predictable expenses (such as monthly rent) and unpredictable expenses (such as an auto repair).

A budget shows income, which is the money coming in, and expenses, which is the money we spend. Expenses can be divided into various types:

- *Fixed.* A fixed cost does not change from period to period, or it changes only very slightly. Fixed-cost items are usually paid every week, month, or year. Examples include rent and car payments.

- *Flexible.* A flexible cost does change from period to period, so it is easily altered or avoided by the person bearing the cost. Examples include heating and cooking gas, electricity, water use, and clothes.

- *Periodic.* Some foreseeable and unforeseeable expenses do not happen on a monthly basis. Examples of foreseeable periodic expenses include birthdays, holidays, and taxes. Unforeseeable expenses include unexpected health problems and car repairs.

Even before we begin writing a budget, we need to get a sense of all these expenses, as well as income. Some people do this by writing down all their expenses every day—whether it is $1.25 in a soda machine or $1,250 for a medical bill. We can also keep all our bills, even after we've paid them, so we have a regular record of expenses. If we are paying via checkbook or credit card, we can keep a record through those as well.

When we create a budget, we list all these things. It is easy to list the fixed costs—we know what they are. And by looking at previous bills, we can get a good sense of what we currently spend on the flexible costs. Periodic expenses can be a little tricky, and this is where a good record-keeping practice really helps. For example, if we know we go to sixteen birthday parties every year and spend about $30 on each, we know we will spend about $480 per year (or $40 each month) on birthday presents. But what about new tires for the car, which we only buy every four years or so? Well, we can still build that cost into the budget. By looking up a price ($480 for four tires) and dividing that amount by 48 months (four years), we can budget for the tires by planning $10 each month. With this kind of foresight, even those seemingly unpredictable costs can be planned for. That way they don't set us back!

Similarly, we need to include the amount we wish to save as a fixed cost. Let take a look at the current spending account for Miguel and Juana, a couple with two children.

Miguel works at a call center, solving computer problems, and Juana works twice a week as an interpreter. Their budget looks like this:

| Total Monthly Income | |
|---|---|
| Miguel's Wages | $1,580.00 |
| Juana's Wages | $600.00 |
| **Total Monthly Assistance** | |
| SNAP (Supplemental Nutrition Assistance Program) | $300.00 |
| WIC (Women, Infants, and Children nutrition program) | $100.00 |
| Child Care Assistance | $200.00 |
| **Total Income and Assistance** | **$2,780.00** |
| | |
| **Total Monthly Expenses** | |
| Paying Yourself First | |
| Retirement Savings | $100.00 |
| **Housing** | |
| Rent | $1,200.00 |
| Electricity | $50.00 |
| Cell Phone | $100.00 |
| Cable Television | $35.00 |
| Internet | $10.00 |
| **Transportation** | |
| Gas | $80.00 |
| Maintenance | $10.00 |
| Insurance | $100.00 |
| Public Transportation | $60.00 |

| Health | |
|---|---|
| Insurance | $70.00 |
| **Food** | |
| Groceries | $400.00 |
| Eating Out | $100.00 |
| **Children's Expenses** | |
| Child Care | $230.00 |
| Diapers | $80.00 |
| **Entertainment** | |
| Movies (including rentals) | $40.00 |
| Pets | $20.00 |
| **Personal** | |
| Clothing | $50.00 |
| Laundry/Dry Cleaning | $10.00 |
| Toiletries | $20.00 |
| Barber/Salon | $40.00 |
| Household Supplies | $20.00 |
| Tobacco | $40.00 |
| **Total Expenses** | **$2,865.00** |
| | |
| **Total Income and Assistance** | **$2,780.00** |
| **Total Expenses** | **$2,865.00** |
| **Balance = Income − Expenses** | **-$85.00** |

We see that Miguel and Juana have listed all their income, including assistance they get from various programs for people with low incomes. In an earlier version of their budget, they had just enough, but they were not paying themselves first by saving for retirement. When they included retirement saving, they saw they would be $85 short of balancing each month. What might they do to avoid this shortfall? This all depends on their personal situations. Juana works only two days a week; perhaps she could pick up more work and earn more money. Miguel smokes, and it costs $40 each month. He could quit and save that $40. He has a friend who cuts hair—maybe he could trade haircuts for his family in exchange for helping his friend with the computers at his salon.

Looking even harder, they realize that in their city, they have good public transportation. If they sold the car, they could save on gas, maintenance, and insurance, about $190 a month. But then their public transportation costs would increase, and Juana would need to have child-care backup for days when her interpreting work took longer. They decide to investigate whether that savings would be worthwhile. They could eat out less often, too, although that is an important part of the way they bond as a family. They could cancel the cable television if they wanted to save more.

Then they realize there are things they forgot to list: Maria wants to start taking dance lessons, and they did not plan for birthday parties, holiday gifts, or any sort of emergency fund. They go back to work on the budget. Each month, they revisit it and adjust by adding in expenses they forgot to plan for and noting where they've found additional savings.

What's important is that Miguel and Juana now have a picture of how they think they are spending and saving. They are now paying themselves by planning for retirement. And when both children are in school, Juana plans to work full-time so they can begin a college savings plan.

The budget is not perfect, and sometimes Miguel and Juana are frustrated. But they've noticed another benefit of budgeting. They used to fight over what to spend and worry about surprise expenses. Now they have fewer surprises and fewer arguments. Even better, they work together to plan for fun expenditures. Later next year they will take their family on a weekend trip. They have started a special savings account for that vacation, funded with the money Miguel had been spending on tobacco.

*Step 3: Understand credit*

"Credit" is a way to buy products or services now and pay for them later. "Interest" is charged as the fee for this service. Examples of credit include credit cards, mortgages, car loans, student loans, department store credit, and medical payment plans.

Credit has benefits and it has drawbacks. Here are some of the good things about credit:

- Credit can serve as a safety net for unexpected emergencies.
- It is convenient: we can use a credit card online or when we travel and need hotel rooms and a rental car.
- It sometimes includes protections against theft or faulty merchandise.
- It can help us track our expenses, since many credit card companies provide reports online that show us how we spent our money each month.
- We can build a good credit history, which helps with major investments such as buying a house or renting an apartment.

But credit has drawbacks too:

- Credit costs money—interest and fees.
- It is easy to overspend: the credit card doesn't seem like real money, and we can tell ourselves it will be easy to pay it back, when it won't be easy.
- It ties up future income. We have to put our money toward paying off the debt instead of using it for savings or other essential purposes.
- It can ruin our credit history if we don't pay all of our bills on time.

If we use credit, we should use it wisely. *That means we use it when we know the thing we spend the money on will ultimately help us generate even more wealth over time.* For example, getting a loan to train for a new job as a machinist is a good investment, because that way we can get a better job and earn more money. Using that same money to buy a brand new car is a poor investment, because the car loses 25 percent of its value the minute we purchase it. Besides education, other good uses of credit include buying a house, buying equipment needed to start a business (when we have a good business plan that shows our business has a good chance of succeeding), or buying a used car that enables us to get to and from work on time. Poor uses of credit, besides buying a new car, include clothing (except uniforms that we must have for our work), electronic devices, and vacations.

Credit costs us money. For example, if we buy a car that costs $4,400 and get a thirty-six-month loan at 12 percent interest (a $150 payment each month), we will actually pay $5,400 for the car ($1,000 more than its purchase price). In general, try to keep credit within these guidelines:

- Housing costs, not including utilities, should be 30 percent or less of your gross (pretax) income. For example, if pretax income is $3,000 per month, seek housing that costs less than $900 per month.

- Consumer debt should be 20 percent or less of your gross income. For example, total consumer debt for a $3,000 per month income should not exceed $600 per month.

- Student loans should not be greater than what you expect to earn during the first year after graduation.

- However, total debt (housing, consumer credit and loans, and student loans) should be 36 percent or less of your gross income. With a pretax income of $3,000 per month, the total debt should not exceed $1,080. (This is why housing and consumer debt need to be looked at carefully.)

Credit cards often carry many hidden charges. The interest rates are usually very high. There may be annual fees and late fees and fees for going over the credit limit. For this reason, it is best to pay off as much of the credit card balance as possible each month. Many people try to pay the entire amount that is due. Also, the credit card payment must be paid on time. If it's paid after the due date, the company will charge late fees, which may be much more than the amount charged.

There are also some very bad credit card companies. For example, some will charge $500 for the credit card membership fee and begin charging interest on the card immediately. That means before we have even used the card, we are paying interest on the $500 fee. This is a terrible deal; no one should do it.

Such a credit card company is an example of a "predatory lender." This term is used to describe loan companies that take advantage of people who are desperate for money. People who are new to the U.S. financial system can easily fall prey to one of these lenders. Be careful of credit card and loan offers that include the following phrases:

- "payday loans"
- "bounce protection loans"
- "auto title loans"
- "rent-to-own"
- "tax refund anticipation loan"

Finally, it is important to know that the financial system in the United States tracks our history of applying for loans, paying bills on time (or not), opening credit cards, and closing them. This goes into a rating called a "credit score." These scores affect our ability to get a new loan and affect the rate of interest we will be asked to pay. A person with

---

### Microloans and lending circles

Two forms of credit that can be helpful for us are "microloans" and "lending circles." Microloans are small loans, typically under $2,500, that are very helpful for starting a small business. For example, like Guillermo, we might use a $2,500 loan to purchase cleaning equipment needed to start a housecleaning business, or to purchase equipment needed to operate as a paid disc jockey for parties.

Lending circles have been in use for many years in some parts of Latin America (for example, *tandas* in Mexico) and are now coming into use in the United States. In a lending circle, a group of people get together and each person agrees to contribute a certain amount at regular intervals for a set time. They also agree that each of them can have the entire amount in a specific order. So, if six people agree to each put in $100 a month for six months, then each month, in an order they determine, one of them gets the entire amount. This can be a very useful way to quickly get enough cash for some purpose, so long as all the people in the lending circle meet their obligations. A recent innovation is that some lending circles may be facilitated by an institution using promissory notes. This makes the lending circle more formal— and also allows each member to quickly build up a good credit rating, because the lending circle contributions show up on their credit records.

a lower score is considered "high risk." Those considered high risk may not be able to get a loan, may be required to make a higher down payment, or may pay a higher interest rate. This is why it is very important that we pay our bills and loans on time. Also, the use of credit scores in the United States is why we should have some sort of credit card, at some point. For example, if we intend to take out a loan to buy a car or a house but we have always paid for everything with cash, we will not have a credit rating. Lack of a credit rating makes it difficult to get a loan.

*Step 4: Pay taxes and use the tax system*
If you earn money in the United States, you must pay taxes. This is true whether you are paid in cash or by check. If you work for a company that is paying you by check, they will be withholding some money from you and sending it to city, state, and federal governments to pay for your taxes. Let's look at Abram's situation as an example.

In Abram's first summer after graduating from high school, he got a job in a warehouse earning $12 per hour, working forty hours a week. He was expecting to bring home $960 in each two-week pay period. When his check arrived, he was shocked to see the amount was only $700. It was less because $147 was taken out for federal taxes, $65 deducted for Social Security, $16 for Medicare, and $32 for state taxes.

The first paycheck with all those deductions can be a shocking disappointment. We all use services, and our taxes pay for those services. The deductions also cover living and medical costs we will incur in the future when we retire. When we are not earning much money, though, systems are in place to credit some money back to us. This is one of many reasons it is helpful to file a tax form every year. Quite likely, Abram will receive a refund from his taxes, especially if he is living on his own (and not a dependent of his parents) or has dependents of his own.

Taxes must be filed by April 15 every year. Even if we do not owe taxes, we should file, because we may be eligible for things like the Earned Income Tax Credit, the Child Tax Credit, the Child and Dependent Care Credit (also known as the Child Care Tax Credit), Education Credits, or other refunds that help people earning lower incomes. These credits can add up. Some of these, however, are only available to U.S. citizens and legal residents.

Even if we are undocumented workers, we can file for taxes. To do this, we need an ITIN number. Tax help is often available for free at local community agencies, and assistance is also available online. Many people find that they get a tax refund at the end of the year. This can be a good way to build up an emergency fund if you put the refund into savings immediately.

Tax-refund advance loans are sometimes offered as an "advance" loan against a refund we *might* receive. *Beware of these!* They may charge high fees and interest rates—they are usually an example of predatory lending.

### HOW TO GET AN ITIN AND FILE TAX FORMS

*ITIN.* An Individual Tax Identification Number (ITIN) enables a person who does not have a Social Security Number (SSN) to pay taxes. Latinos in this country without papers can still obtain an ITIN from the Internal Revenue Service (IRS). The IRS is prohibited by law from sharing information regarding taxpayers with other governmental agencies. *This means that it is illegal for them to report an undocumented taxpayer to other agencies, including the Department of Homeland Security and its USCIS branch.* The ITIN also enables a person to use the banking system in many states, obtain a mortgage, and establish a record of residency and taxpaying. This is useful on its own, and may become helpful as immigration reforms are enacted and people are allowed to apply for legal status. Information on obtaining an ITIN can be found online at www.irs.gov/Individuals/Individual-Taxpayer-Identification-Number-(ITIN). The form, labeled W-7, requests specific types of supporting proof of identification, biographical information, and a tax return. You can apply directly or file with a certifying acceptance agent who can help. A toll-free IRS help line is also available at 1-800-829-1040 in the U.S. in Spanish and English. (Outside the U.S. the number is 1-267-941-1000; this is not a toll-free number, so the call will involve a fee.)

*Taxes.* Tax forms are available online, at libraries, and at other locations. Many community agencies offer help filing taxes during tax time. Volunteers who understand the tax system provide help filing. A variety of commercial sites also offer help, but these will charge fees. And the reality is that many people's taxes are not that complicated and don't require professional help. It is not necessary to use an accountant or a paid service, except for complicated taxes involving businesses.

For online tax help, always start with the IRS, www.irs.gov, and its toll-free phone number, 1-800-829-1040. Other helpful IRS programs, Volunteer Tax Assistance (VITA) sites (1-800-906-9887 toll-free) and Tax Counseling for the Elderly (TCE) sites (1-888-227-7669 toll-free) are offered in many communities. Call their numbers to find locations near you.

If you have trouble with the IRS, Low Income Taxpayer Clinics (LITCs) are independent organizations that provide low-income taxpayers with representation for free or a nominal charge. These clinics also provide tax education and outreach for taxpayers with limited English proficiency.

*Step 5: Use the banking system*

Banks and credit unions are safe in the United States. A *credit union* is like a bank except it is a nonprofit organization and does not earn profits for the bank's owners. Because of this difference, credit unions sometimes offer slightly better rates and customers may be treated a little better. Banks typically offer a wider range of services and may have more branch locations than credit unions do.

Money stored at home can be stolen, destroyed by fire, or simply lost. Money deposited in the bank or credit union is safe from theft, loss, and fire. In addition, if a bank or credit union would fail, the deposits we've placed there are insured for up to $250,000 per depositor. Banks and credit unions also are convenient. With our bank or credit union accounts, we can use debit cards or paper checks. We can bank electronically on the Internet, making it easy to pay bills and make purchases. Checks from employers can be transferred by direct deposit—deposited electronically—into the bank or credit union, which saves us a trip and makes the money available immediately. And having an account at a bank or credit union saves the expense of using check-cashing services. Finally, having a bank account helps us develop a savings record, which builds our credit history.

To open an account, a person needs to provide the following information:

- name, address, date of birth
- a Social Security Number or ITIN (described earlier)
- a government issued photo identification (ID) card, such as a driver's license, passport, or photo identification from home country

Savings institutions compete with each other and offer different rates, so it is a good idea to compare the costs of their services and the interest rates they pay on accounts. Here are some things to consider when choosing where to do your banking:

- fees, such as a monthly service fee, check-printing costs, fees for overdrafts (when you spend more money than you have in the account), ATM withdrawal fees, and fees to receive a canceled check

- the initial deposit required and the minimum balance you must keep in the account

- interest rate paid on savings or checking account

- whether the bank will take a direct deposit from an employer

- convenience and accessibility

- quality of customer service

The checks deposited in a bank are not always immediately available, because the check has to "clear," or be processed, first. So if a friend writes us a personal check for $300 and we deposit it, we may not have access to the cash from it for a few days.

Savings institutions offer a number of different types of accounts. The account that is best for one person may not be best for another, so it pays to explore the options.

*Savings accounts* usually pay interest on the money deposited. These vary in the amount of interest paid, the minimum amount to be kept in the account at all times, how frequently we can withdraw from them, and other factors.

*Checking accounts* allow you to write checks to pay bills or to give money to other people. Some checking accounts pay interest, but others do not. With a checking account, you'll get a supply of paper checks and probably a debit card (also called a check card), which is handy for in-person payments. If you make a check card payment or write a check for more money than you have in the account, it will "bounce" and you will incur an overdraft fee. Checking accounts usually give access to an ATM machine. Some ATMs charge money for withdrawals but other do not. You must balance your checkbook by recording all the checks and debit charges against it, as well as any fees charged, subtracting payments, withdrawals, and transfers, and adding deposits.

*Certificates of deposit* (CDs) are a form of savings that pay higher interest. However, CDs require that you don't use the money for a certain amount of time and usually involve larger deposits of money. If you withdraw the money early, you will pay a penalty.

Sometimes the bank may close an account because we have overdrawn it, or taken out more money than was available. To reopen an account, talk to the bank or credit union. Typically one must pay the balance due, offer to directly deposit paychecks, open a savings account, or have a friend or family member open a joint account. If the savings institution still denies the account, you are entitled to a free checking verification report and to correct any errors.

---

### Questions to ask before opening an account

- What is the monthly fee for maintaining this account?
- What is the minimum balance for this account? Is there a fee if my balance drops under that limit?
- What is the interest rate on my savings account?
- Is this account insured?
- Are there limits on the number of deposits, withdrawals, checks, or ATM uses per month? What fees apply if I go over my limit?
- Where can I withdraw money without paying any fees? What fee will I be charged if I use an ATM machine that doesn't belong to this bank?
- Is direct deposit available for this account?

## Which are better: credit cards or debit cards?

The answer depends on how you use the cards.

*Credit cards* are helpful because you build credit and the cards can offer some perks. Using credit cards, however, carries the risk of getting you into debt, because it is easy to spend money you don't have.

*Debit cards* are helpful because you can never overspend: the money comes directly from your account. And you don't have to worry about interest, late fees, or paying a monthly bill. Using a debit card is definitely the safer option.

If you spend more money than you have, you're going to run into trouble no matter what card you use. So it's important to use your credit and debit cards wisely. Here are pros and cons of each. The items in common are printed in gray type.

|  | Debit card | Credit card |
|---|---|---|
| **Pros** | ▪ Easy and convenient<br>▪ Online and paper statements allow you to track your spending<br>▪ Safer than carrying cash<br>▪ Useful for paying bills online<br>▪ Allows you to spend only the money that you have in your account<br>▪ Useful at ATMs to withdraw cash when needed<br>▪ Frequently requires no application or starting fee | ▪ Easy and convenient<br>▪ Online and paper statements allow you to track your spending<br>▪ Safer than carrying cash<br>▪ Useful for paying bills online<br>▪ Protection from theft and fraud<br>▪ Short term loan to help pay for things right away<br>▪ Using it builds credit<br>▪ Usually offers perks or benefits like cash back or air miles |
| **Cons** | ▪ Very limited protection against theft and fraud<br>▪ Doesn't improve credit when you use it | ▪ Too easy to spend money you don't have<br>▪ Interest charged is throwing away money<br>▪ Must pay monthly bill; missing payment or paying late hurts your credit and requires fees<br>▪ Application necessary |

*Step 6: Understand the costs of ownership (for example, when deciding to buy a vehicle)*

After buying a house and paying for a college or technical education, a car is typically the most expensive purchase the average person makes. Often we've dreamed of owning a certain type of car, and we think that having that car will be a dream come true. It may or may not be that way in reality. Automobiles are always more expensive than they appear. They require insurance, maintenance, and gas. And they lose value quickly. It is certainly more practical to think of a car as an appliance, like a washing machine or an oven, than as a symbol of success or a dream come true. But not many people are able to view a vehicle that way. Let's look at how Victoria went about buying a car.

Victoria has been in a secure job for three years. She is tired of taking the bus to work and decides it is time to buy a car. She is considering three cars from different dealers, each asking a different down payment:

|  | 2013 Chevy Cruze | 2005 Ford Escape | 1999 Toyota Camry |
|---|---|---|---|
| **Purchase price** | $22,430.00 | $12,235.00 | $5,675.00 |
| **Down payment** | $2,200.00 | $1,200.00 | $2,000.00 |
| **Monthly payment, 5% interest, 5-year loan** | $385.54 | $208.24 | $69.35 |
| **Total price for car** | $25,332.00 | $13,694.00 | $6,161.00 |

It is immediately clear that the total price is very different for each of these cars. She does some investigating and learns that the Cruze and the Camry each will get better fuel economy than the Escape, so she rules out the Escape. She has never owned a car and the Cruze is really pretty. In contrast, the Camry looks worn, although it is in good shape for its age, according to her uncle, who says that model is known for lasting a long time. But he also says he thinks the price on the Camry is too high, and that it is so old it could easily break down.

Victoria is falling in love with the Cruze, but she realizes the monthly payment will be 35 percent of her income. She could afford that now while she lives at home, but in a few years she hopes to move out. The choice is hard! Victoria goes to the library and does more research. She's not ready yet and needs to learn more. She begins to look at the cost to insure different kinds of cars, which cars are cheaper to operate, and how much it will cost her to park her car downtown for work. She realizes that for her first car, it might be better to start with something older, since she may make some mistakes. At least she has a better idea now of how to think about purchasing a car, even if she hasn't made her mind up yet.

Victoria had stumbled upon an important idea. Before purchasing a used or new car, it is best to consider the *total cost of ownership:*

- price of the vehicle (new or used)
- taxes and license fees (taxes depend on the price of the car; license fees can depend on the age and make of the car)
- price of a loan (a person's credit rating and the type and age of car affect the interest rate to be paid on the loan)
- price of insurance for that vehicle (some cost more to insure than others)
- fuel use (cars with better fuel economy use less fuel and are cheaper; some cars require premium fuel, which is more expensive)
- maintenance costs (some cars have more expensive parts than others, for example, the tires on a big truck cost much more than the tires on a small commuter car)
- vehicle's depreciation: the amount of value the car loses between purchase and resale (New vehicles depreciate the moment they are purchased. The largest drop in value happens in the first three years of ownership. And some brands and types depreciate faster than others.)

That list of expenses shows that a lot of things go into the total cost of ownership. Many publications can help you learn more about the costs of owning a vehicle. *Consumer Reports,* which can be found in most libraries, explains which cars are more reliable. *Kelley Blue Book* (www.kbb.com) describes typical prices for new and used cars and also provides helpful information on the total cost of ownership. What exactly goes into those costs of ownership? Over a five-year period, here's the average for all vehicles:

- fuel: 26 percent
- insurance: 9 percent
- state fees: 6 percent
- financing: 6 percent
- depreciation (loss in value over five years): 44 percent[33]
- repairs: 4 percent
- maintenance: 5 percent

A good rule to follow is that the total cost of owning a car should not exceed 20 percent of a person's income. The consideration should be made while looking at the entire household budget—not while at the dealership, where the cars all look so good and where the dealer's only interest is selling you something. Start with the household budget, consider what the family needs, and then weigh what the family *wants*. Then begin investigating which vehicle will meet those criteria. It is better to buy a car with cool head than to fall in love with it as though it's your "baby." The good news is that good values are always out there, and with patience and persistence we can find a vehicle that meets most of our criteria.

The fact is that most of us are not aware of all the hidden costs involved when we look for cars. We tend to be excited by the look of a car and think it says something about how wealthy or stylish we are. It's good to know that some very wealthy people in the United States drive plain, old cars, because a car is not a good place to invest money. We may have a vision of pulling up to the basketball game in a Jaguar dressed in fur coats. That's fine, but we may need to go through a few rusty jalopies while we build enough money to afford that particular dream!

*Step 7: Begin to build assets*
The final step in financial literacy is to begin to build assets. An "asset" is a tangible or intangible item that increases one's wealth. For example, an education and a home are assets. The total value of all of our assets is called our "net worth."

Let's discuss in more detail some of the assets that help build wealth.

**Education that contributes to job placement, retention, or promotion.**
Even though it may cost money to pursue a certification or degree, if that degree enables us to attain a new job, advance in our career, or retain our current position, it is money well spent. A recent study of technical, short-term degrees and certificates (usually one- or two-year programs) and college baccalaureate degrees showed that both can deliver good value. In some cases, the (less expensive) short-term degrees paid for themselves more efficiently than the he longer-term degrees. The choice of degree makes a big difference, and degrees involving technology, engineering, and mathematics are especially valuable.[34]

### Savings accounts

As we noted in the section on budgets, we should always pay ourselves first. It is possible to set up multiple accounts. For example, we can save for education for ourselves and our children; we can save for a home down payment.

### Retirement savings

Most of us will need extra money to cover our retirement. Many employers offer 401K and similar retirement savings programs that automatically deduct money from each paycheck and invest it in a retirement account. The interest on these investments compounds over time. By starting to invest while young, a person can accumulate quite a lot of wealth.

Consider two people, Lola and Luis. At the age of twenty-two, Lola begins putting $100 a month into a mutual fund that grows, on average, at 8 percent per year. She quits investing after only ten years and lets it grow. This means she has put in $12,000 to the account. Luis, meanwhile, waits until he is thirty-two and starts putting away $100 a month in the same type of account. He keeps doing that for thirty years, so he will have put in $36,000. At age sixty-two, who will have more money—Lola, who only put in $12,000, or Luis, who put in $36,000?

The answer is Lola, because she started younger! The total value of her account will be $234,600, while Luis's will be $177,400. *It is better to start saving a small amount early and be disciplined about it than to wait and try to save a larger amount later.* At the same time, it is never too late to start saving.

It is better to make regular savings and retirement savings automatic, by having a small amount withdrawn from each paycheck. If we withdraw savings regularly, we get accustomed to the take-home pay and forget about the money that is invested in savings and retirement. That's how it should be. And we should never touch the retirement savings until it is time to retire.

### Equity investments

Some of us also invest in the stock market. Books and classes can teach us about how to invest. These investments can be risky. The benefit of these types of investment is that some may grow quickly or steadily and pay off well. However, unlike with savings, the money is not protected and can be lost if a stock or mutual fund performs poorly. Some people form investment clubs. They get together and thoroughly research various stocks and mutual funds and decide which to invest in.

### Home and other real estate

For many of us, a home is our most important asset. The loan, called a "mortgage," can cost quite a bit of money (making the house a liability for a time). But eventually, when we have paid off the loan, our only costs will be taxes, insurance, maintenance, and utilities. Plus, we can eventually sell the home, and we may get more money for it than we originally paid. Other real estate, such as vacation land or homes, may also add to our net worth. Some people use real estate as a business, buying apartments or houses and renting them out or fixing them up for resale.

Holding on to a home can be difficult in tough economic times or when we lose a job. Losing a house, called "foreclosure," occurs if the mortgage loan payments aren't made as scheduled. Foreclosure prevention is designed to help people keep their houses during these difficult times. Many community housing agencies offer help. Most lenders do not want to see people go bankrupt, foreclose on the mortgage, and lose a home, and may make arrangements to slow or delay payments until a new job is found.

### Businesses and business equipment

If we own our business, even if it is part-time, the business and its equipment can add to our net value. If operated correctly, the business brings in income, but it also adds to our value if it is a type that has assets and can be sold. For example, even businesses that rely on a service, such as carpet cleaning, can be sold—not just the equipment, but the valuable client list and the knowledge about how to run the business effectively are valuable assets.

Many credit unions, banks, and other financial institutions offer advice on building net worth over time. Classes are also available through community education.

## Summary: Chapter 5—Making a Living

We feel better when we have work that rewards us, whether we're working in the home taking care of our family, in an office, on a construction site, or elsewhere. We know that through work, we contribute to our personal well-being, the well-being of our family, and that of the larger community. Learning to speak English and maximizing our education are two major ways we can improve our access to good work that pays well. And when we are earning money, we need to develop the skills to manage that money well, protect and increase it, and use it to help our families do better.

Questions to think about:

- If I need to continue learning English, where do I go or who can teach me?

- If I need to learn new skills, where to do I go and who can help?

- What are my financial goals?

### *Reflection questions*

1. If I moved to the United States from another country, what are some things I have to learn when I'm living here?

2. If I need to continue learning English, where do I go or who can teach me?

3. What are the most useful words or phrases to know in English to navigate life in the United States? Why are they important?

4. Do I know about opportunities available to advance my education, to obtain a high school, college, or advanced degree?

5. What skills, and talents am I proud of? (List them.)

6. What job did I have in my country of origin? Can I find similar work in the United States? Or do I have to consider a change?

7. If I need to learn new skills, where do I go? Who can help?

8. What are my financial goals?

9. What organization in my area can help me make a plan for saving money safely?

10. Do I know my credit score? Where can I get information about establishing or improving my credit?

11. Where do I find information about such things as opening a bank account or buying a car?

### Resumen: Capítulo 5—Ganándose la vida

Cuando tenemos un trabajo que nos recompensa nos sentimos bien, ya sea que trabajemos en el hogar cuidando de nuestra familia, en una oficina, en una construcción o en otra parte. Sabemos que por medio del trabajo contribuimos a nuestro bienestar personal, al bienestar de nuestra familia y el de la comunidad en general. Aprender a hablar inglés y ampliar nuestra educación son dos formas importantes de mejorar nuestro acceso a un buen empleo que pague bien. Y cuando ganamos dinero, debemos crear las destrezas para administrarlo bien, protegerlo e incrementarlo, y usarlo para ayudar a que nuestras familias vivan mejor.

Preguntas para reflexionar:

- ¿Adónde me dirijo o quién me puede enseñar si debo continuar aprendiendo inglés?

- ¿Adonde me dirijo y quién me puede ayudar si necesito nuevas destrezas?

- ¿Cuáles son mis objetivos financieros?

CHAPTER

···six···

# In a Foreign Country

## *At a Glance*

This chapter is especially for and about first-generation immigrants to the United States, although it can also help their children, friends, and loved ones deepen their understanding of what it means to be an immigrant. The act of immigration—from the decision through the long period of adaptation to our new home—can be very challenging to any human being. Other issues that arise in the United States, such as crime, discrimination, and the experience of being an unauthorized immigrant, can complicate life and emotional well-being. In this chapter, you will learn about some of the issues surrounding this transition:

- what kinds of trauma can result from immigration
- strategies for adapting to being a "foreigner"
- how discrimination and crime affect us
- some ideas about the meaning of "being bicultural"

"I CAME HERE FROM MEXICO with an American Dream," says Leonardo. "But once I got here, I woke up to a different reality. Fitting into society is hard. Being undocumented is a major problem. It is hard to find work, and you can't feel free. You don't have the same opportunities as other people. The language is a huge barrier. You feel like you are being judged everywhere you go and every time you speak.

"I feel completely bicultural. I am comfortable in my home country and comfortable here in the United States. I can navigate both cultures. I adapt my behavior depending on the context. Of course, there's a negative side to this. In a way, I never feel like I totally belong to my country of origin or my U.S. home, even after thirteen years here. And the longer I am here, the more I realize how different I am from the dominant culture. Yet there are so many values of this culture that I love—and some that I don't like at all. Then I go back home and there are things I love there, and things that I reject. In one sense, I am not at home in either culture. And in another, I know myself better than ever as a result of understanding where I came from and where I am now."

The United States is the world's leading destination for immigrants. Some of us come to this country seeking financial stability. We may come to earn money and hope to send it home, pay for a house to be built, and then return home one day. Some of us come because we feel we have no choice. We may face problems such as oppression, crime, and violence that make life unbearable and make it impossible to raise children safely. Some of us come because we can pursue our professional choices in the United States.

Regardless of how and why we come—and whether we intend to live here for a few years or the rest of our lives—we all face issues while trying to adapt to U.S. culture. These issues affect our mental well-being, generating both happiness and sadness. This chapter is especially for first-generation immigrants to the United States. We will cover some of these issues surrounding adaptation:

- what kinds of trauma can result from immigration
- strategies for adapting to being a "foreigner"
- how discrimination and crime affect us
- some ideas about the meaning of "being bicultural"

### Immigration as a traumatic episode

A child awakes in the middle of the night, suddenly afraid of what might be in the closet. All he sees is a dark space. He can't see into the space, and his imagination begins to run wild. Soon he imagines monsters and cries out for his parents.

If we have not had this particular experience, we have likely experienced something similar. All humans fear the unknown. As adults, we may fear fewer things than we did as children, but there are a great many unknowns and we still face many fears. A fact about the experience of immigration is that, though it may feel exciting, it is marked by many unknowns and the fears that accompany them. These unknowns and fears persist for months and years and provoke feelings of anxiety. The experience of anxiety over months or years is hard on people. As immigrants, we may experience anxiety at the time of our decision to leave our home, at the moment of saying good-bye, during our crossing into the United States, and as we learn to navigate life here.

This does not mean immigration is bad for us, or a horrible thing, or something we never should have done. Many immigrants are pleased with their choice and the out-come of it. Many do not experience the difficult situations we will discuss in this chapter. However, it is important that we acknowledge there are stresses tied to the experience of immigration, and some of these stresses can live as shadows in our lives for some years. By being frank about the fears and negative experiences we have endured, we can bathe these shadows in light and gain a greater sense of well-being. Some of these issues were covered in chapter 3, when we discussed various emotional challenges. Here we review some specific aspects of immigration that may induce trauma. Should we find that these experiences are overwhelming us and making it difficult to think, work, sleep, or be with other people, it is a good idea to seek help from a counselor.

### The decision to leave

Some of us are brought here as babies or children. Among those of us old enough to act on our own, the decision to leave is sometimes forced by conditions of oppression or violence that mean that our very lives, or those of our families, are in danger. Or desperate economic conditions may bring us to the decision that, for the good of others or ourselves, we need to seek better opportunities elsewhere. Often a period of time occurs between the moment we make the decision and the moment we act on the decision. This time is a period of quiet anxiety. No one really knows what we are going through.

One counselor put it this way: Put yourself in the place of young diver about to jump from the ten-meter board for the first time. You have heard stories about people who did not jump right or landed sideways or on their belly and were hurt. Will that happen to you? You walk to the edge, look down at the distant water, and realize you are about to fall the height of a three-story building. Now you jump. No one is with you. In the silent moment when you leave the board, you know there is no turning back. There is only the unknown. You have no control. What will the water feel like? Will you land sideways? Will you remember how to do everything right so you are not hurt?

Of course, with a dive, you fall quickly, you hit the water, and the wait is over. You either did it right, or you didn't, and your body tells you soon enough!

But imagine if that moment of falling lasted not a few seconds but months. This is the experience of immigration. For some immigrants, we can add to this quiet, lengthy anxiety the extra stresses of limited money, lack of legal documents, and guides we do not know or trust.

That was true for Alonso, from Nicaragua. "I knew I had to leave my country," he said.

■■■ *My children had little to eat. I decided I would go to the United States, where I had some cousins who were working and sending money home and who said they knew of jobs for me. My children and wife would stay with her parents, and I would send money back. It was a sad decision, but I felt excited, too, knowing that I would start on a new adventure and that I would be able to at least do right by my children.*

*I had heard many horror stories and these kept me awake at night. People dying, being locked in trucks, getting abused by bosses, being caught by authorities, or losing a parent and being unable to get back home to grieve their loss with family.*

*I reassured myself that none of these things had happened to my cousins. I kept my fears and worries to myself. I did not want to trouble anyone, and it was not right for me to burden them anyway. They were going to have their own hard time. They were being left too. I gritted my teeth and prepared myself for anything.* ■ ■ ■

It is quite normal for people to hide their anxieties and fears. However, it is important for us all to understand that this period of "silent time" between our decision to leave and the beginning of our transition can be stressful *even when we are unaware that it is stressing us*. It is hard for others to see that we are having a traumatic experience, and even hard for us to realize this time is traumatic. Psychologists have learned that when humans experience a period of intense fear, they can experience a severe reaction that causes them emotional difficulties later on. This is true even if the person primarily feels excitement, happiness, or sadness during this period. Feelings of desperation may be circulating underneath these other, more familiar feelings. Counselors at CLUES have seen that the real trauma of this period often does not become apparent to people until several years into their life in the United States. Counseling and therapy can help people overcome the problems associated with fear and trauma.

### Saying good-bye and crossing

Eventually it is time to implement our plan, and the transit begins. The moment of saying good-bye is something every person can empathize with. It is always difficult to leave loved ones. Some of us leave unsure of whether we will ever be able to return, for financial or legal reasons. This heightens the sadness.

The crossing itself is quite stressful. For immigrants who come with documents, the stresses are more about the coming unknowns of living in a new country. For those who come without documents, the fears are numerous and continuous. What happens if I don't make it? What happens if I'm caught? What happens if the coyote kidnaps us? The risks and dangers in these crossings often put people into a survival mode. People in this mode "split" the frightened side of themselves off to one side so they can deal with the current dangers. They may see people die, be left behind, or suffer assaults, but while seeing this, they may not react. This is not because they are insensitive people; it is a way to protect oneself from immediate threat.

The trauma of such crossings may be buried by the person who experiences it. When the trauma finally emerges, the psychological pain is almost unbearable. It is not unlike the pain a person experiences when feeling returns to a numbed limb. As the person remembers what happened, they can find it difficult to function normally. (This type of trauma was described in chapter 3: recall Christina, who had nightmares about losing her son.)

### Arrival and early adjustment

Finally we arrive in a new place, and everything here seems different.

That may be true even if we've been here before. As one recent arrival put it, "I had been to the United States many times as a visitor. When I moved here, I realized that I'd always had people to help with the simple things. Then I had to mail a letter. I went to the mailbox four blocks from the apartment where I was staying. I could not figure out how to open it! I waited twenty minutes for someone else to come open the mailbox, so I could see how it was done. Everything was like that. Simple things were complicated."

On first arrival, everything is hard to understand. It takes time, and we need help learning to navigate the systems here. Taking the bus is a challenge. If we are here without papers, the fear of being found out haunts us. Those of us who are the sole support for our families also live in fear of being deported, leaving behind dependent family members who have no means of support. We may become immersed in the struggle to survive.

### Adapting to life as a foreigner

Most of us arrive knowing someone in the United States. That person helps show us the ropes here. Even so, we find that, as with our friend trying to learn how to open a mailbox, everything is different. The adaptation takes a lot of energy. It can be both exciting and frustrating. The lessons are unpredictable and sometimes funny, too, as this English teacher recalls.

> ■■■ *One of my ESL students had gotten work in construction. He didn't have a driver's license, and to save money, he went everywhere by bicycle. He was getting around okay, except for when he asked for directions. People would tell him, "Turn north here, take Thomas Street southeast." When he told us about the problems he was having, we learned that in his home region, nobody used compass directions. They said, "Turn left at this intersection, and then turn right here." We had to explain*

*to him how to navigate by using north, south, east, and west. So it wasn't that he needed to learn the compass directions—he knew what they meant already. The whole concept of using them for directions was new.*

*Every one of my students has funny stories about the meanings of things. One of my student said, "What is it with all these doorways that promise 'success' (exito)?" Of course, he already had figured out that the signs meant "exit." Still, it was a good laugh for the class. One of the funniest was a woman who wanted to know what the meaning of the English word "wuhchadewing." It took us a long time to figure out she meant "What are you doing?" She was actually pronouncing it pretty close to the way many Americans do, slurring the words all together as though it were one word.* ■ ■ ■

Adaptation is painstakingly slow. Sometimes, the people we think are going to help us—the family or friends who came here before us—are not as helpful as we hoped. It is shocking when we arrive and connect with them to see how much they have changed in response to the dominant culture. Often they simply can't help us because of the demands of living here. They may be working two jobs and have little time to see us.

Sometimes they tell us to "tough it out." This can shatter our sense of safety and family, because they are the one thing we have to hold on to. It seems as though they are saying, "I had to go through this; now it is your turn." It is difficult to tell whether they mean to help or hinder, but some have said they take this position so that the newcomer will learn the ropes more quickly. As one counselor said, "To help, they make a decision not to help."

"Toughing it out" is not the best idea. We need direction and help adjusting, and it is better to get that help than to fumble about. Research has shown that two important aids to adjusting are forming relationships with people in the community and learning the language.[35] Next, we will consider various strategies that CLUES clients have used to adapt to life in the United States.

### Strategies that help us adapt

What are the most important steps to take as a new arrival? Let's look at some of them.

### Learn the language

At CLUES, we feel it is very important to learn English as an early step in understanding how to navigate systems. We covered this thoroughly in chapter 5, which explained that

ESL classes usually include information on how to navigate U.S. systems. So a basic strategy to improve adaptation is to attend ESL classes as soon as possible after arrival. Even if we've been here ten years and can get around our neighborhood fine in Spanish, these classes can help open doorways to other experiences. ESL classes often include many types of immigrants—not just Latino—which offers the opportunity to meet new people and learn about other immigrant experiences and ways of adapting. Mastering any language takes a long time. It is one thing to be able to ask for directions, purchase what you need, and "get by" in a foreign tongue, and quite another to be able to express oneself fluidly.

*Settle in a community with other Latinos*

Many large cities and some smaller ones have "little Mexicos" (or "little Cubas" or "little Puerto Ricos") where people all speak Spanish and we can find the things we like. A benefit of these communities is that we can quickly connect with people who will help us learn "the ropes," and we can find something like home. This helps us feel secure as we gradually put down roots. In these areas, we find radio, newspapers, retail stores, restaurants, grocery stores, and other services that cater completely to Latinos. Through these, we can learn about work options, social services, churches, places to live, and other necessities and luxuries. Some would say that a downside of settling in a community like this is that it is more difficult to reach into the rest of U.S. culture. However, others disagree with this. It's a matter of personal goals. In some of the areas of largest migration, there is little need to adapt to the dominant culture.[36] In less urban areas, where many immigrants come to work in agriculture or food industries, we may still find areas of Latino settlement, but these are smaller and offer fewer options.

One resident of an area in Minneapolis that is almost entirely Mexican and Central American said:

> ■■■ *I know many people who stay within a one-mile radius of this neighborhood, and they are happy that way. They know everyone here. If I suggest to them that they go to a restaurant or shop further away, they say, "Why would I want to go there?" The radio is in Spanish, the newspaper is in Spanish, and everything you learn about is the news from Mexico. There isn't even much information about what's going on in the*

*rest of the city and state. For me, this is a form of isolation, but on the other hand, it does create community.* ■■■

### Connect with appropriate services

Many cities have a variety of social services that can help immigrants adjust. These services can help with shelter, mental well-being, child care, education, legal needs, and other issues. They often can help connect people to other needed services as well.

### Find a religious center

Besides their role in facilitating our spiritual life, houses of worship are excellent places to meet people and begin to make oneself at home in a community. In cities with concentrated Latino populations, some churches cater completely to Latinos. Others offer some services in Spanish. Beyond that, the church can serve as a cultural hub, connecting us to events that we enjoy, foods that are familiar, and services that understand the needs of immigrants.

The member of one congregation said,

> ■■■ *I have seen many people who were not very religious back home come to the United States and get involved in church. Faith helps us find reassurance that there is some sense in our decision to come here. Being in church helps. It reaffirms our sense that there is a greater plan. Some of the masses and songs are in Spanish and some are in English. Even when the services are in English, you feel affirmed that your kids are learning values that you want them to learn.* ■■■

### Join parenting groups

For those of us who have children, parenting groups are an excellent way to make connections with other parents and to reach out beyond our close circle. Many school districts offer parenting courses through the schools or through community education courses. Expectations of parents are quite different in the United States than they are in some of our countries of origin. At times, things that are acceptable to us can be unacceptable in the United States. Although we may disagree with the expectations and rules here, we need to learn them. (More information on this was covered in chapter 2.)

*Volunteer in school*

Most U.S. schools welcome parent volunteers. Participating in the school's Parent Teacher Association or Organization (PTA or PTO) is one way to become involved. There, parents can meet other concerned parents and help raise money for school improvement projects. And there are many other ways to volunteer for the schools: we can help in the library, accompany students on field trips, teach about our home country and its culture and foods, or help the teacher.

*Participate in sports*

For many people, especially men, sporting events—most especially *fútbol*—offer a chance to connect to others and a way to remain connected to something we loved about our home country. As one middle-aged man put it,

> ▪▪▪ *You see so many guys playing soccer. It's a way to socialize. Some of us will do* anything *not to miss our weekend* fútbol *with friends. You see guys in their teens and guys in their sixties there. It feels like home, and it is fun.* ▪▪▪

*Consider community involvement or political activism*

U.S. communities offer many ways to be involved. At CLUES, we have especially noted that Latinas benefit from joining and contributing to the work of women's groups. For many Latinas, this involvement becomes about making lives better for the next generation. In Latin American villages, the women all know and support each other, but they may lack some of the women's rights that are available in the United States. In these women's groups, Latinas in the United States are organizing to learn about and assert their rights.

Many children of immigrants have become involved in efforts to change the laws around immigration status. Large-scale deportation has led to greater political involvement in general. One resident of a rural Midwest town described it this way:

> ▪▪▪ *Some people in our town were rounded up and deported. They had been brought in to work at a meat packing plant. It created a huge rift in the town, with children who were born in the United States left behind, some people hiding in fear, some local people angry about it, and others glad. After that, we got active. The families that stayed started to have meetings with the police. We started to report incidences*

*of discrimination and abusive treatment. We started a Spanish newspaper. We educated people and got to know the local authorities. We said, "This is our home too." Community activism is a channel for acculturation. You can either continue to be isolated or you can start from your neighborhood and friends and begin to make change happen. It's not about adjusting to the culture that's here; it's about adjusting the culture itself.* ■ ■ ■

### Discrimination and crime

Experiences of discrimination, crime, and violence complicate our efforts to adapt to the United States. This is even more complicated when we don't have documents. One woman put it this way:

■ ■ ■ *It is tricky. The police don't speak Spanish, and it seems that they don't pay attention to our calls. They may say they will send someone and then they don't. Or the dispatcher may say, "I don't speak Spanish. Have someone call who can tell me what's going on." You hear so many stories. I talked to a woman whose husband was beating her and threatening to kill her, but the police wouldn't come. Then you see the news about a white woman whose husband was jailed for the same thing, and you feel like if you are a minority, you won't get help.*

*I married a man from the United States and came from Spain to live in his home-town, a small city that had very few minorities. My English wasn't bad, but in my first job in a shop, every time I offered to help a customer, they would ask for "the American girl." I looked just as white as everyone else. But when I opened my mouth, people would say, "Why don't you just go home."* ■ ■ ■

Bias and discrimination are facts of life in the United States. Some places are welcoming and other places are unwelcoming. Crime is also prevalent in the United States, especially in low-income neighborhoods where many immigrants settle. In some cities, police are responsive, but in others they are not. Some areas are quite liberal, and some are not. These are realities that we have to deal with. Most of us have experienced discrimination at some point.

Undocumented workers report abuses from employers and others who threaten them with deportation if they do not comply. For example, employers have demanded sex from workers under threat of deportation. Or they have refused to pay for work performed. These acts are illegal. If they occur, the victim has the right to press charges. In some cases, immigrant victims of certain crimes may be granted a U visa, which grants temporary legal status and work eligibility for up to four years.[37]

Stories such as these can make us hesitant to seek help from authorities. When a crime occurs, the best thing to do is to call 911 and report the incident to the police. The police can help the victims and get them to a hospital. The police are not allowed to ask for documents, and you do not have to provide them to get assistance.

Reporting the event and seeking help can also be complicated by language and cultural barriers, as one counselor describes here.

My client's son was being abused by his father. She took him to the authorities to report on the abuse. The boy was afraid to talk to them. "They're strangers, Mama," he said. "I don't want to tell them."

■ ■ ■ *So my client said to her son, "If you talk to them, I will take you shopping for a toy."*
*Immediately the authorities stopped the process. They told her they could not take a report. When she asked why, they said that her offering to get him a toy made it sound like she was bribing the boy to make a claim against his father.*
*I tried to explain to the authorities that this was normal for that woman and her culture, but they would not proceed with the case.* ■ ■ ■

### Be prepared

We don't have easy answers to help deal with these situations. Access to an advocate or translator may help. That's why it's good to get to know the local social service agencies. The best advice is to *be prepared*. Even before any problem arises, ask friends and neighbors about places where they have found help. Learn whether these places have Spanish speakers. Visit the agencies and ask what programs and services they have. That way, if you ever have a problem, you are already prepared to seek help from the right people.

Pressing for help from authorities who seem deaf to our troubles is exhausting. Yet there is no other way. This is where community involvement and activism can begin to make a difference. When groups representing the community get to know the local authorities and seek allies who can help exert pressure on them, change happens. The process takes a long time.

---

### Sexual assault

Sexual assault is an act of violence that occurs when one person makes another person part of an unwanted sexual act by using either physical force or coercion. Sexual assault can happen to women and men of any age, race, ethnicity, sexual orientation, and socioeconomic class. Here are some examples of such violence:

- rape by someone the victim knows or by a stranger
- incest
- prostitution
- sexual harassment (unwanted touching, words, and sexual gestures)
- other abuses

Many myths are told about sexual assault:

- *"It is the victim's fault."* Sexual assault survivors are never to blame for the actions of a perpetrator.
- *"Sometimes 'no' means 'yes.'"* When someone says "no" to sexual relations, there is no consent.
- *"She asked for it. Look at how she is dressed."* No one asks to be sexually assaulted. The clothing one chooses to wear is not a substitute for consent to sexual activity.
- *"Sometimes the woman should submit to having sex."* A woman never owes sex. Both people must consent before engaging in any sexual activity.

#### Your rights

Regardless of citizenship or immigration status, anyone who is a victim of sexual assault or any other crime has the right to file a crime report.

---

**Finding legal help**

When we are seeking help with immigration status, criminal justice, housing, discrimination, or unfair employment practices, legal assistance is essential. Laws vary from state to state, and so do the systems for seeking help. If you are near an area with many Latino immigrants, start your search for help there. If you are using the Internet or a phone book, try looking for terms like these:

- "Legal Assistance" or "Legal Aid" (usually with your state's name, as in "Illinois Legal Assistance")
- "Volunteer Lawyers Network"
- "Lawyer Referral Service"
- "Immigrant Law Center"

Some online sources include these:

- National Immigration Legal Services Directory (www.immigrationadvocates. org/nonprofit/legaldirectory)
- U.S. Immigration Support (www.usimmigrationsupport.org)
- Legal Services Corporation (legal aid for low-income Americans, www.lsc.gov)

## The idea of being bicultural

"I hear many people who always talk about 'going back,'" says Bianca. "But the joke from others is, 'Once you're here, you're here. Don't even think about going back, because you are not.'"

Counselors at CLUES regularly hear from clients whose dream is to send enough money home to have a place there to retire. Some of them manage it. But it takes a long time, and in the meantime, they set down roots in the United States. They marry, have families, and their children are fully "Americanized." Yet inside, they feel the tug of "home" all the time. Other stories throughout this book shared some of these feelings, the unsettled sensation of living between worlds. We go home, and old friends now see us as American. But back in the United States, Americans see us as foreigners, even when we've been here much or our lives.

The position of being of two worlds affects everything about us—our sense of identity, how we view our family, our emotional well-being, and our sense of spirituality. The strategies for adapting discussed earlier in the chapter and elsewhere in this book can help. At a certain point, many of us begin to feel that we are "bicultural" or "multicultural."

Getting documents is a big issue and can help us feel more that we belong where we are. Tobias recalls,

> ■■■ *I came to the U.S. at the invitation of my father who was naturalized and offered to help me get papers. Things got messed up somewhere along the line. They sent the paperwork to him but he'd moved. In the meantime, I got on with my life, met a woman, fell in love, had children. And always this was nagging at me. Finally I got papers, and then I officially married the mother of my children. It was a huge thing. My oldest son was mad at first. He had known his parents weren't married but was ashamed to talk about it with his friends. But by the day his mother and I married, that was a different story. He was beaming. The burden of this secret was lifting from all of us. It was a very happy day.* ■■■

The issue of legal status is an important one in the process of feeling at home in the United States, but by no means the only one. About half of the legal immigrants from Latin America and the Caribbean choose to become naturalized citizens, according to research by the Pew Hispanic Center (now called the Pew Research Center's Hispanic Trends Project). This rate is lower than the rate for immigrants from other parts of the world, about three-fourths of whom choose citizenship. Those Latinos who do naturalize cite acquiring civil and legal rights, including the right to vote, as the main reason. Other reasons include having access to the benefits and opportunities derived from U.S. citizenship, family reasons, viewing the United States as home, and wanting to become citizens. In the same research, Latinos who haven't tried to become citizens cite personal barriers, such as a lack of English proficiency, and administrative barriers, such as the financial cost of naturalization.[38]

The longer we are here, the better we become at navigating and benefiting from the culture that is here. But we are also prompting the mainstream culture to adapt to us. It's a balancing act, says Elsa:

▪▪▪ *A friend told me that where she works everyone talks in Spanish. We talked about whether they should be speaking English. She likes it that they only speak Spanish and wants to keep it that way. But some people say, "Break with that, that's the old way, adjust to the new world." She says, "What do we do with the people who don't speak English? We can't all change in one day. It's not practical. We have made a community here where you can do everything in Spanish. We have to honor the spirit of the community. People, English speakers, come from all over the city now to shop and eat here. We wouldn't have this if it weren't for the language."*

*I agree with my friend. We have to honor the culture we are bringing to this place. You cater to the mainstream culture, but you also have to cater to the Latino culture.* ▪▪▪

### Taking pride and finding strength

The idea of being *bicultural* is double-edged sword. It means we can be comfortable in both cultures. We can navigate both, and we intuitively adapt our behaviors based on the context. The other side is that you never feel as though you totally belong to either culture.

"I am happy here, but I also have come to realize how different I am from the dominant culture," said one woman a decade after immigrating. "There are things I appreciate and have internalized, and there are other things I'll never understand. But it is like that when I return home too. So it is like I am comfortable in both, but not one-hundred percent a part of either. The downside is that there is a sense in which I am never really at home in either place. I am a foreigner in both cultures...I feel a little disconnected from both."

Many of us find strength and pride in our country of origin. We follow our favorite sports teams, know the politics, and watch our shows. For most of us, language and food help us maintain pride in our history, and these are things we pass along to our children. But we also pass along our own success by helping others. One young man called it a "chain of hope."

▪▪▪ *Mexicans in this town have Cinco de Mayo as a big deal. They celebrate roots, being united, and this gives them hope. But many other things give strength and pride. We like helping one another. We like supporting our schools.*

*For me, the passion of wanting to be somebody, to be a part of things, motivates me and gives me strength. When someone who is newer here asks me for help, it makes me happy to give some of my knowledge to someone who is going through what I went through. It will be like a chain of hope. That's why I take pride in my work in helping people. And I see others, landscape workers, for example, who take such pride in the quality of the work they do and how it makes the neighborhood look beautiful. And others who came here not knowing how to do construction and are now looking to become their own bosses.*

*It is not easy to adapt and to become comfortable. It takes time and courage. But it is a great source of pride to realize that we've learned the language, have a good job, fit in, and can laugh, cry, and talk with people who treat us like equals.* ▪▪▪

When talking with friends, we'll say, "Back home we do it this way," and we know that our friends understand us. But even though we think of "back home" as somewhere else, "home" is where we are now. We can take pride and find strength in both places.

## Summary: Chapter 6—In a Foreign Country

Each Latino immigrant adapts to the U.S. culture in his or her own way, especially when different regions offer varying options for maintaining the home culture. Immigrants also change the culture of the place they've moved to. But there are some shared experiences and strategies that help many people feel more comfortable here. The immigration decision and journey can affect a person's mental health, and being honest with ourselves about these experiences is helpful. People use various strategies to adapt, including settling in areas with many other Latinos, learning English, and developing relationships through church, volunteering in the community, or playing our favorite sports. Admittedly, crime and discrimination can harm us. They can threaten our personal safety and also our feelings of identity and emotional security.

As we explore the idea of becoming bicultural, we can appreciate the huge variety of ways in which people navigate life in their adopted home.

Questions to think about:

- What is my story of immigrating to the United States?

- What did I do, or what can I do, to adapt to life in the United States?

- Do I feel more comfortable in one culture over another, in both, or neither?

### *Reflection questions*

1. What is my story of immigrating to the United States?

2. Are parts of the story too scary to think about?

3. Do parts of the story remind me how strong I am and the obstacles I am able to overcome?

4. When did I first think about immigrating to the United States? How old was I? Was it even my decision?

5. What kinds of thoughts and feelings did I have when I was preparing to move?

6. Do I have someone to talk to about my experience, such as a friend, a priest, or a counselor?

7. What did I do, or what can I do, to adapt to life in the United States?

8. Have I felt discrimination? How does it affect me?

9. If I have experienced crime, whom did I ask for help? What was the result?

10. What programs and agencies do I know in my community that can help me feel protected?

11. Where do my friends and relatives go when they are in trouble with legal issues?

12. What culture or cultures am I a part of? Do I feel more comfortable in one culture than another? Comfortable in both cultures? Or in neither? Whom can I talk to about these thoughts and trust with my feelings?

## Resumen: Capítulo 6—Fuera de mi tierra

Cada inmigrante latino se adapta a la cultura de los Estados Unidos a su manera, especialmente cuando diferentes regiones ofrecen opciones para mantener la cultura de su país de origen. Los inmigrantes también cambian la cultura del lugar donde se radican. Pero existen experiencias y estrategias compartidas que ayudan a muchas personas a sentirse más a gusto en este país. La decisión de inmigrar y el viaje pueden afectar la salud mental de la persona, y es muy útil ser sinceros con nosotros mismos acerca de estas experiencias. La gente usa varias estrategias para adaptarse, incluyendo radicarse en zonas con mucha gente latina, aprender inglés, tener amistades a través de la iglesia, ser voluntarios en la comunidad o practicar nuestros deportes favoritos. Por supuesto, la delincuencia y la discriminación nos pueden perjudicar. Pueden amenazar nuestra seguridad personal y nuestros sentimientos de identidad y seguridad emocional.

A medida que exploramos la idea de ser bicultural, podemos valorar la amplia gama de formas de como la gente se adapta a la vida en su hogar adoptivo.

Preguntas para reflexionar:

- ¿Cuál es mi historia de inmigrar a los Estados Unidos?

- ¿Qué hice o qué puedo hacer para adaptarme a la vida en los Estados Unidos?

- ¿Me siento más a gusto en una cultura que en otra, en ambas, o en ninguna?

CHAPTER

··· seven ···

# Drawing Strength and Joy from Our Spiritual Life

## At a Glance

We Latinos are very diverse people, but almost all of us feel that some form of spirituality is an important part of our lives. In this final chapter, we explore some of the ways people approach the concept of *espiritualidad* and how it can be a source of strength and peace in our lives. You will learn a bit about these topics:

- how our shared history as Latinos is tied to our approaches to spirituality and religion

- how we draw strength from our sense of spirituality and the community, especially as we deal with issues of acculturation

- how spirituality allows us to see good aspects in bad situations

- how spirituality can help us through difficult times

- how we can negotiate differences in our beliefs within families and communities

"WE MUST ALWAYS THINK OF GOD FIRST," says Anita, a ninety-four-year-old great-grandmother, when asked for her advice to others.

"I used to worry all the time about everything, and I used to make every little thing a big problem," says Placido, who found his spirituality by participating in Alcoholics Anonymous. "Now I take it easy. I ask my Higher Power for guidance, and things just seem to work out. The answer comes to me, maybe through something someone else says, or through something that happens."

"My friend approached me to talk," says Justino, a pastor and theologian. "He was worried, because his daughter was dating a boy who was an atheist. He did not think the boy would be good, but I said to him, wait, and watch, and get to know this boy. Keep an open mind. Talk to your daughter and find out what she sees in him. Don't jump to conclusions that he is bad simply because he does not believe as you believe."

Although Latinos are very diverse, almost all of us share a strong sense of spirituality and a deep connection to family, which are critical to our well-being. But the concept of "spirituality" needs to be thought of in the broadest terms, as exemplified by Anita, Placido, and Justino. These three Latinos all have a sense of spirituality. One places God at the center of everything. Another has found, through participation in Alcoholics Anonymous, a sense of Higher Power, through which he has found a life that works much better for him than his previous life. The third is a pastor, and yet he advises a friend to look for the good in a young man who does not believe in God.

Some people describe our shared Latino spirituality as a "sense of transcendence." This means most of us believe there is a world beyond that which we see, touch, taste, hear, and smell. We think there is a reason and order to the universe, even if we cannot always understand it. We feel, as though they were still with us, the spirits and thoughts and love of our family and friends who have passed on. This sense of transcendence is important to the mental well-being of many Latinos. Many of us find that spirituality is a bridge between the challenges we face and our feeling of safety and security in the world. Spirituality helps us find a context for our challenges. We see that those challenges are a part of something bigger than ourselves.

Our sense of spirituality can be observed in many customs, sayings, and beliefs:

- We have a common belief that "Whatever you do will come back to you, because the universe does not hold anything." This impulse moves parents to do good things, knowing that even if they will not benefit, one day their children will harvest the fruit of the parents' efforts. This same belief helps people avoid things that are wrong, such as cheating, even when they know they could get away with it.

- Many of us continue to speak to our parents, grandparents, and siblings long after they have passed away. We can talk with them and know they are hearing us. Some of us have a sense that they are always with us—not in our imaginations, but truly with us.

- Our faith in God remains firm even when bad things happen to us, even when those things are done by someone who claims the misdeeds are done in the name of God. We separate the human institution of religion from the transcendent nature of God.

- We have a strong sense that things happen according to a larger purpose. Often in conversation among Latinos, one will hear the phrase *"si Dios quiere"*—"if God wants it." This sense lets us value what we have now, even if what we have is not what we want. It gives us an appreciation of the moment.

- Many of us pray every day, even those of us who do not go to church often or follow any particular religious teaching.

- Many of us have religious objects in our homes and attend religious services at least once a month.[39]

- A majority of us believe that miracles are performed today just as they were in ancient times.[40]

Latinos celebrate spirituality through various religious traditions, but many of us feel that religion is not the same as spirituality. Religiosity focuses on such things as church attendance, specific creeds, regular reading of the Bible or other religious texts, and participation in religious rituals. Certainly these are important to many of us, but beyond those practices, spirituality is about the deeper meaning of events and our relationship with our concept of a universal supreme being or high consciousness.[41]

In the United States, almost seven out of every ten Latinos (68 percent) identify themselves as Roman Catholic. Latino Catholics make up about one-third of all Catholics here. Fewer than two of every ten of us (15 percent) identify as Protestant, and less than one in ten (8 percent) do not identify with any religion.[42] The numbers convey what we sense: to us, God feels like an active force in our everyday life.

A great many of us attend religious services in Spanish or with other worship characteristics related to our Latin American roots. Three-quarters of Latinos who were born outside the United States attend a Latino-oriented church, as do about half of those who were U.S.-born. Surveys show that we tend to see religion as a moral compass that guides our political thinking, and that we expect this of our leaders.[43]

In this chapter, you will learn a bit about Latino spirituality, including these aspects:

- how our shared history as Latinos is tied to our approaches to spirituality and religion
- how we draw strength from our sense of spirituality and the community, especially as we deal with issues of acculturation
- how spirituality allows us to see good in bad situations
- how spirituality can help us through difficult times
- how we can negotiate differences in our beliefs within families and communities

### A shared religious history

Our shared history is tied to our approaches to spirituality and religion. The indigenous peoples of South, Central, and North America had their own spiritual traditions. The Catholic church was a principle force in colonizing portions of North America and most of Central and South America. Catholicism was forced on the indigenous peoples in lands colonized by Spain and Portugal. Catholic missions were established by the

> **Learn more about Latinos and spirituality**
>
> In 2006, the Pew Research Center's Hispanic Trends Project conducted in-depth surveys and research on the religious beliefs of Latinos. More than 4,000 Hispanics participated in the survey. The results, published in 2007, paint a fascinating picture of our religious and spiritual preferences and beliefs. To learn more, download the entire report, *Changing Faiths: Latinos and the Transformation of American Religion* at www.pewhispanic.org/files/reports/75.pdf.

Roman Catholic church to aid in the conversion of indigenous peoples and in the purging of native belief systems. These missions also worked to change native agricultural and nomadic practices and to steer indigenous people toward a more European manner of life. The missionaries established schools, model farms, and hospitals. When some Europeans questioned whether the indigenous people were truly human, Pope Paul III in 1537 confirmed that their souls were as immortal as those of Europeans and that indigenous people should not be robbed or made into slaves. Some missions in Latin America helped prevent colonialists from making slaves of the indigenous people. So although the church had a prominent role in the conquest of indigenous people and the suppression of their cultures, it eventually helped protect them.

Indigenous beliefs blended with some aspects of Catholicism. For example, the celebration of *Nuestra Señora de Guadalupe,* Our Lady of Guadalupe, who first appeared to an Aztec Indian in Tepeyac, Mexico, is considered by some scholars to be blended with the worship of the Aztec Goddess Tonantzin Coatlalopeuh. This goddess had been worshipped by the people at a temple in Tepeyac prior to European conquest. The Virgin of Guadalupe is a powerful religious and cultural symbol for many people because she represents God's loving, maternal, and comforting characteristics. Moreover, she appeared to an indigenous person rather than a European, and so the Virgin of Guadalupe is also a symbol of the survival of a people and resistance to oppression. She shows that God did not abandon them.[44] The importance of the Virgin of Guadalupe to many Latinos, especially those of Mexican origin, can be misunderstood by outsiders, who don't realize that she symbolizes multilayered cultural and spiritual values. Many men and women feel a personal relationship, through prayer, with the Virgin of Guadalupe.

Africans who had been brought to the New World brought their spiritual traditions with them. These blended in with Catholic traditions, but are still practiced today. Santeria, one of the better-known traditions, is practiced in Cuba, Puerto Rico, Dominican Republic, Costa Rica, Colombia, Venezuela, and the United States. The religious tradition of Candomblé, or Macumba, developed in Brazil and practiced in Uruguay, Argentina, Venezuela, Colombia, and Panama, is a similar blending of Catholic and African religious practices.

Liberation theology emerged in in the 1960s out of the injustices against marginalized peoples in Latin America. It emphasizes love and compassion for the suffering experienced by impoverished and oppressed people. The concepts underlying liberation theology—that love, justice, and equality are inseparable and part of the core teachings of Christianity—have become important to many Latinos. One result is that surveys of U.S. Latinos show that they are more likely to endorse a combination of religion and politics than non-Latinos. Two-thirds of Latinos say their religious beliefs influence their political thinking, and more than half say that houses of worship should address social and political questions of the day.[45]

Although Catholicism remains the most-practiced religion among Latinos, there is a growing movement of born-again or Evangelical Protestants, as well as charismatic Catholics. This approach especially emphasizes God's ongoing, daily intervention in human affairs.

Our goal is not to describe the complex spiritual and religious history of Latin America, but to help explain some shared history that shapes the views of many Latinos. Although non-European religious beliefs (those of indigenous Americans and Africans) were suppressed, they blended with European beliefs, which helps explain why the religious traditions of Latinos have a different tone than those of the dominant culture, even when they are of the same denomination. A strong feeling that there is a world that transcends this one accompanies our religious practices. Also, although the church was at first a tool of oppression, it later came to protect indigenous people. So its role is complex, but it includes a political or "worldly" role that persists into the teachings of liberation theology. Finally, there is a sense that the universe is a loving, compassionate place, as opposed to an impersonal, cold place. We express this sense in a variety of ways and religions.

**Drawing strength from spirituality and religion**

The experience of immigration is shared by almost all Latinos. As a result, many of us feel a sense of displacement—a feeling of living in two worlds at once and of not being quite at home in either world. The feeling of being "split" between worlds creates tension, as we've described elsewhere in this book. One immigrant from Colombia describes the feeling this way:

> ▪▪▪ *Many of us came intending to stay and work and then return. An indicator of this is that through history, other immigrant groups in the U.S. brought their own religious leaders with them. They intended to build a new home here. We did not; ours stayed in our home countries, and we found churches and priests and ministers here, but often they were not Latino. Then we have children. And we realize we need to stay here for them, and develop our own religious leaders. But a result of this is that we have one foot in our old country and one foot in the U.S.* ▪▪▪

The feeling of being a part of two worlds is very common among Latinos. First-generation immigrants have left behind much to move to a new place and create a better future for themselves, and more importantly, for their children. They have a strong sense of identification with their home country, but living in the United States, they become more like the people of the mainstream culture. We hear this from our old friends and family when we go home to visit. Latino children born in the United States, or raised here from an early age, are perhaps caught between two worlds even more than their parents. They are in many ways American, yet those in the mainstream culture still see them as foreign, and their parents still see them as part of their own country of origin. So the echo of the old country is strong in the second generation, and it continues to echo for generations. One might describe this experience of having "feet in two countries" as a strong feeling of being tugged in two directions by the powerful orbits of two planets.

Religion and spirituality are both important aids to coping with the sense of being pulled in different directions. Religion offers a place, practice, and cultural hub where we can find other people somewhat like us who have similar experiences. This helps us feel that we belong with others, and it affirms our identity. (And as you'll recall from chapter 1, personal identity is important to our mental health.)

Even if we feel torn between two places, we still know that we are a member of a religious community, or as one elder told us, "a child of God." Spirituality helps us find the security that things will be okay, despite the tension of being pulled in two directions at once and despite the discrimination or other issues we face. This is because we know there is a higher purpose to our life experiences.

"Church has been so important to me and to my friends," explains one lay leader of a Latino congregation. "Some of us have families that have been split up by deportation. Families where there is only one parent who is working two jobs and trying to get the kids to all their school and doctor appointments. Families affected with PTSD—post-traumatic stress disorder. Parents who saw their children die in their arms. They deal daily with language issues, discrimination, rejections, legal challenges, and struggles over how roles are changing in the house and how kids behave in the U.S. At least at church, we can deal with these issues among others who understand."

Many churches are important sources of practical assistance. More than half of Latinos (sometimes as much as 84 percent) say they have found assistance with food, clothing, finding employment, financial problems, housing, child care, and language or literacy training through their place of worship. Latinos also find volunteer opportunities through their churches.[46]

Efren Maldonado is a staff member of CLUES and the pastor of church that serves a primarily Latino congregation. He finds that Biblical stories can help people understand the situations they are facing in a wider context. In his words:

■■■ The members of our church are still grieving the loss of family, friends, and possessions left behind when they decided to come to this country in search of a better future. Then the process of acculturation distorts the roles within the family. Parents end up depending on their children's ability to speak the language. The parents feel that they no longer have authority, and they lose their self-esteem. Children may be born in the U.S. and identify as Americans, yet their non-Latino peers ask them where they are from.

Latinos in general live in alienation and marginalization. We move to the U.S. because this country promises opportunity, but it also presents a lot of barriers. Most Latinos are stuck living between two worlds, and while they can see the promises of *a better life in this new land, they have to battle against the giants of discrimination, racism, social injustice, and oppression. This battle has byproducts such as self-hatred and low self-esteem.*

*The story of Exodus and Moses' story provide a helpful analogy here. Born Hebrew and raised by Egyptians, Moses faced struggles and issues of identity similar to those faced by many Latinos. Moses was forced to flee as an adult, and he came as a refugee to Midian where, despite marrying, being warmly received in his father-in-law's household, and having a child, he was never able to identify with his new community. He even gave his son the name Gershom, which means "foreigner." This is the same feeling experienced by immigrants in general and first-generation Latinos in particular. This feeling never goes away completely.*

*The Scriptures are a source of strength and encouragement in our journey of understanding and as we embrace our role in this new place. Moses was a multicultural man, and God used Moses' skill in multiculturalism to free the Hebrew people from slavery. Latinos and other immigrants need to know that the God of Moses remains the God of the immigrants. God will be with us in our entrances and exits. God will not only help us with our personal situation but will assist us with our responsibility toward those in need.*[47] ■ ■ ■

Churches that focus on the needs of Latino immigrants play an especially valuable role in helping first- and second-generation Latinos adjust. We feel comforted when we are with others who, at minimum, speak the same language. And even more so, we find in such churches people who have had similar experiences to ours. This is not uncommon for people who only attended church occasionally in their home country. In this way, churches that cater to Latinos provide many benefits. They serve as a cultural hub, connecting us and helping us find comfort through each other, reassurance about a shared past and a hopeful future. They can help us connect to the various services and information we may need as we adjust to life and to new challenges. As with the story of Moses, Biblical stories often contain wisdom that helps us better understand the challenges we face. And for many of us, a church is, of course, an important conduit to our spiritual selves and a balm for our aching souls.

### Spirituality helps us find the good in the bad

Many people in the United States are very individualistic, with a belief that we are each responsible for our own successes, accidents, and failures. According to the American Dream, if you work hard and are ethical, you will get what you want, and it is yours alone to do with what you want. It is your success. You built it. The converse is that if you somehow don't get what you want, or something bad happens, then it is your fault and it is your problem to deal with.

Many Latinos see life differently. Our sense is that we do our best, and whatever happens at the end of the day is what is wanted by God (or by the universe or our Higher Power or by whatever constitutes the transcendent world). This is a subtle difference that some people miss. Our sense of "whatever happens will happen" does *not* mean that we abandon plans to improve our lives and "leave it up to God." Just look at the evidence: we came here to make things better for ourselves, so obviously, we believe that we can do things to improve our lives. Our faith means that we understand that we are not in control of the *outcome* of our efforts. We can only control our efforts and the way we respond to the outcome. We make the plans and do our best, and what happens, well, that is in God's (or something else's) control, not ours. That's what Pilar learned as a high school student.

Pilar was in the top ten in her class. She had good college entrance test scores, was a top athlete, and had a record of volunteering at several agencies to help elders in the community. She had done everything the school counselors had advised to get into the very best universities. She had researched scholarships and financial aid, and her mother and aunts and uncles were prepared to help her with tuition. But the only school that accepted her application was her "fallback" choice, a state college in a small town. She was devastated and cried to her mother and father. "You will see," they said. "Something good will come. There is something better for you."

Now three years in, Pilar looks back on the time she was so devastated. "Mami and Tío were right. I love it here. Those other schools were too big for me. I would have felt lost at them. I know all my instructors, and they have helped me so much. They've helped me line up internships and connections, and I already have job offers for when I graduate. The people here care about me. And I've made good friends. It all worked out for the best."

Some people view Pilar and her parents' way of interpreting events as naive, as though they are looking back and using hindsight to make the best of not getting into the colleges she had wanted. But for many other people, the way that Pilar's family made sense of events is a strength that is deeply tied to their faith. They believe there is an organizing principle in the universe that is loving and wants the best for people.

It is difficult to explain this interpretation to a person who grew up in a very individualistic culture. To Pilar and her family, it is simply a fact that despite our best efforts, none of us can control how things turn out. We simply can do our best. Pilar had done her best, and she was not accepted by the schools she had dreamed of. Her family had faith that there were better things to come for Pilar and that they would work out. They have interpreted the event in a way that brings great comfort and security. Quite probably this interpretation even helped Pilar get so much out of her "fallback" college choice, because she went there with a positive spirit instead of a sense of disappointment. Our belief that things will happen "as God wishes" helps us maintain hope and motivation. This is one way of describing the Latino perspective.

Of course, it is a generalization to say "These people believe this, and those people believe that." But as Latinos learning to live in the dominant U.S. culture, it helps us to understand that, in general, we are more likely to see events a part of "plan" for a positive universe. We can feel secure knowing that things will work for the best. Our spirituality helps us make sense of a world that is sometimes disappointing and sometimes dangerous. In Pilar's case, that sense enabled her to cope with disappointment and seek the best in her college education. In this way, spirituality is a great aid to mental health and to living with life's challenges.

### Spirituality en tiempos malos

Many if not most of us Latinos have faced traumatic events. As we noted in chapters 3 and 6, the very act of deciding to leave home (or of recognizing that one has no choice but to leave) creates a traumatic internal situation. This trauma continues as we make our crossing and often persists in daily life in the United States, where we may face unfair treatment by employers and legal authorities and bias from all kinds of people. This is especially the case for those of us who are here without papers. We may live with daily fear of being discovered and endure horrific and abusive treatment in order to protect ourselves from deportation. Often we endure this not so much for ourselves but for the family members who have become dependent on us. That was Estella's dilemma.

Estella was referred to a mental health clinic after she had endured severe physical and emotional abuse from her husband. Although she was worried for herself and her children, she also believed that a marriage vow was sacred. She was scared, too, that if she complained to authorities she would be deported and her children, who were U.S.-born, would be under her husband's vicious rule.

Her therapist helped her talk about the situation. After listening to her and developing a relationship with Estella, the therapist said, "Tell me, Estella, do you believe in God?"

"Of course I do," said Estella. "I pray day and night for God to change me or change my husband so that the abuse will stop."

"Do you think God wants you to be happy or unhappy?"

"Well," said Estella, "I think maybe God wants me to be happy."

"Do you believe that God is perfect?" asked the therapist.

"Yes, I believe that. God's creations are perfect."

"So," said the therapist, "do you think that God would be so cruel as to create humans to be like puppets, to be pulled about as though on strings? To be abused?"

"God is not cruel," said Estella.

"So, here you are in this situation. You are unhappy and you are being abused. Is that really consistent with God's ideas? Is it possible that God might want you to be free of this situation?"

"That might be," said Estella. She agreed to talk more with her therapist about the situation she was in, practical things she could do to protect her children and herself, and how God might be an ally to her in finding a better path.

As we deal with difficult situations, our underlying sense that God is a positive force can guide us. At the same time, we have to keep in mind that the churches and other places of worship we use may have interpretations or religious positions that we don't agree with. And that can create conflicts, as one couple found out.

*Diego and Maricarmen's story*

Diego and Maricarmen were anxious and depressed. Their wonderful daughter Diana had recently told them that she was a lesbian. It was hard for Diana to tell them. She did not want to hurt her parents, but she had learned from them that honesty helps keep a family together. She explained that she had waited to tell them until she was very sure, but that she could not keep this a secret from the people she most loved, the people who had brought her into the world.

The couple was glad that Diana had told them. They told Diana that they had always loved her and would always love her and that they respected her for being direct with them. Later, Maricarmen confided to Diego that she had often wondered if this was the case, and to her surprise, Diego said he had wondered as well. They smiled to each other about that. They had been married a long time. Theirs was a partnership and family rich with love, and they knew each other and their daughter well. Still, it was not easy to realize that some of the things they had dreamed of would be changing, now that the truth was on the table.

Soon they became very serious. Diego recalled that their minister had preached many times that homosexuality was a sin. Diego said he had always grimaced inside when the minister went off on that subject, even before Diana came to them. Diana was a good person. She was not a "sinful" person. She was first in their eyes. They were so torn. They had been members of the church for fifteen years. They had helped it grow from a few members to close to one thousand. They had donated time and treasure to see it succeed. They had helped bring in the new minister, and they had welcomed him to their home many times. They had pushed for services that used music familiar to parishioners. This church was like their home!

Should they leave their church? Were they hypocrites if they stayed? Would they be disloyal to their daughter if they did not leave? But why should they leave the church that was, after all, their extended family, where they had so many friends and had found so much joy? How could a place that had been the source of joy also be telling them there was something wrong with their family? Were they being unfaithful to their minister's teachings if they stayed? The more they talked, the sadder they became, full of questions and doubts.

They decided that at some point they would discuss their thoughts with their minister. But they were not ready to do this yet. They needed to think more, and they needed to talk to close friends first. So Maricarmen and Diego went to talk to their compadres Blanca and Augustine. Maricarmen knew that they had been through something similar. They talked all Saturday and half the next day.

Augustine finally said, "Look, we do not know what is right for you and your family. And our church is a little different than yours, although we have heard some of the same stuff from people at our church. And we have not played the same kind of important role in our church. But for me, a church is a human thing. It can help with finding God, but they are not the same thing. When Blanca and I went through this, we had to come to terms with that.

"I cannot say what is right for you," he continued. "But I can say that Blanca and I love our child as you love yours, and we feel that we can be faithful to our church even when sometimes it feels as though it is not faithful to us. It is our faith in God that has helped us learn to live with that paradox. We know that God is with us in hard times and in good times."

### Respecting differences in spiritual traditions

In the United States, many churches emphasize a personal relationship with God, and this may follow from the U.S. emphasis on individualism. However, whether Latino or native-born U.S. citizens, most people tend to celebrate special occasions and give special attention to spirituality through participation in a church, synagogue, mosque, or other place of worship. With such great diversity among Latinos, there are many differences in how we practice and what we believe.

These differences challenge us. Research into Latino beliefs discovered that although three-fourths (76 percent) of Latinos hold favorable views of Catholics, only half (49 percent) are favorable toward Evangelical Christians, 44 percent are favorable toward Jews, 42 percent are favorable toward Pentecostal Christians, 32 percent are favorable toward Mormons, 27 percent are favorable toward Muslims, and only 19 percent are favorable toward atheists.[48] This research suggests that a number of us hold biases about other religions. Although we grew up in our own diverse cultures, the United States is even more diverse. Our children and grandchildren will be friends with and perhaps marry people from many different faith traditions (or no faith tradition). What happens to our beliefs then?

For many Latinos, the relationship to God is a communal activity, and celebrating with others is a part of spirituality. Yet in today's world, there are many different kinds of people and different ways of seeing things. The experiences of Diana, Diego, Maricarmen, Blanca, and Augustine are good evidence of this. Justino, the pastor who counseled his friend to get to know his daughter's atheist boyfriend, had other things to say about differences, even among people in the same congregation:

> ■■■ *When we make faith so personal, we risk losing our sense of community and God. The truth is that relationship to God should be communal. God came to reconcile the world, the whole community. Community is based in love and is inclusive. Yet each person in it is unique. I believe each one of us has a function. I don't think we should all be the same. Even conflict between people is part of the process that God uses to create new things. Differences are a part of God's design. They are not negative.* ■■■

Still, what about the daughter who is dating the atheist? Her parents have legitimate concerns. If they get married, will the children be raised the way the parents raised their daughter? What will they do about baptisms? Holidays? Can their daughter be married in a church? And what about when Diana finds a woman to love, marry, and bring forth a new generation? These are not simple questions to answer, especially when we place such high value on family and on spirituality.

Similar questions occur for families when an engaged couple are of different faiths. And no doubt about it, the questions create stress for the families. Yet these differences can usually be worked out within the family. As Blanca and Augustine said to Maricarmen and Diego, the church is a human thing. Families find many ways of resolving these differences. Placido, the elder who found his sense of spirituality through participation in Alcoholics Anonymous, explained that his mother was Catholic and his father was an atheist. Justino, in fact, is from a Caribbean family in which one parent was Baptist and the other had been raised in a family in which the father sometimes attended Santeria rituals. These differences will always be with us. They are going to increase as time passes.

Sometimes families need help working out successful ways to bridge the waters that separate us, and relationship counselors can help us figure out these resolutions. One CLUES therapist had this to say:

■■■ *I have seen conflict come from the practical implications of mixed marriages. When children arrive, how do you decide? What I help these couples with is what I do with any other conflict. I help them learn how to talk about the difference, negotiate it, and make agreements. But to me, these differences are not about spirituality. Sometimes people grab hold of religion as a way to protect themselves— they may fight for religious beliefs without exploring what's really going on underneath. You might say they cling to the regulatory aspects of religion without exploring the underlying principles. Part of the process couples go through when negotiating these differences is to connect with spirituality and be less concerned about the religiosity. But I find that most people are generally familiar with the distinction between the two.* ■■■

Ultimately, says Justino, these differences are gifts that help us learn to support each other:

■■■ *When you are unique, you bring something no one else can. That is what makes you special. But your uniqueness means that you can't bring everything. This means you are also dependent. Someone else has something you need. This dependence is what creates relationships in a community. We help each other, and we support each other. Being unique and coming to the realization that we depend on others allows us to be what we are meant to be—and to be a support to each other.*

*I do not want to say this is a generalization that applies to all Latinos. It is what I have observed, and what I think helps people learn to live with their differences.* ■■■

## Summary: Chapter 7—Drawing Strength and Joy from Our Spiritual Life

Spirituality binds us together. Like the love of family, it is a value shared by almost all Latinos. Spirituality and the ways we practice religion help us adjust to life here. Spirituality can be a great aid when we are struggling and suffering. Spirituality can help us see the best opportunities when we face disappointments. We have many differences in religions, and as our children and grandchildren branch out into this large world, we will encounter more differences. Yet even when the differences seem to be about religious or spiritual matters, our spirituality can strengthen us, our loved ones, and our community.

Questions to think about:

- What do I experience when I think about God or a Higher Power?
- Whom do I talk to when I feel that I'm doing something against my religious or spiritual beliefs?
- Do I find a connection with other Latinos based on our common beliefs?

### *Reflection questions*

1. Is spirituality a part of my life?
2. What do I experience when I think about God or a Higher Power?
3. What activities or religious practices make me feel at peace?
4. Are there times when I don't feel understood in the new country?
5. Do I trust that there is a reason for my current struggle?
6. Whom do I talk to when I feel that I'm doing something against my religious or spiritual beliefs?
7. What happens when I share my spiritual beliefs with someone who has different beliefs?
8. Do I ever have doubts or worries about my beliefs?

9. How do I regain a strong sense of faith after it has wavered?

10. Do I find a connection with other Latinos based on our common beliefs?

**Resumen: Capítulo 7—Sacando fortaleza y alegría de nuestra vida espiritual**

La espiritualidad nos une a todos. Al igual que el amor a la familia, la espiritualidad es un valor compartido por casi todos los latinos. La espiritualidad y las formas de practicar la religión nos ayudan a ajustarnos a la vida en este país. La espiritualidad puede ser de gran ayuda cuando sufrimos y pasamos dificultades. La espiritualidad nos ayuda a ver mejores oportunidades cuando enfrentemos desilusiones. Tenemos muchas diferencias en lo relacionado a la religión, y a medida que nuestros hijos y nietos abren su camino en el mundo, encontraremos más diferencias. Aún cuando éstas parecieran ser sobre temas religiosos o espirituales, nuestra espiritualidad nos fortalece a nosotros, a nuestros seres queridos y a nuestra comunidad.

Preguntas para reflexionar:

- ¿Qué siento cuando pienso en Dios o en un poder superior?
- ¿Con quién puedo hablar cuando siento que estoy haciendo algo contrario a mis creencias religiosas o espirituales?
- ¿Encuentro una conexión con otras personas latinas basado en nuestras creencias en común?

# Conclusion
## Personal Well-being, Family Well-being

WE HAVE A SAYING *Haz el bien sin mirar a quien*. Do good without looking to see who benefits. This is a fine saying with many layers of meaning. It indicates that we have faith that whatever good we do—at some time and in some place—will benefit someone. That what we do matters. That goodness is enough.

This saying tells us something about the way we value ourselves as a part of something much bigger. This belief is a potent force in the lives of Latinos.

It tells us that regardless of whether we are religious, most of us have a strong sense of the universe as a good place. We do our best, and we know that eventually the people we care about will benefit. We are part of a bigger world.

That feeling starts at home, where we are loved by so many people. We learn that many people care for us, and we learn that our role is to care for them too. We derive much pleasure and satisfaction from seeing them do well.

As with all things, there is another component to this belief. We cannot *do* our best if we ourselves are not at our best. Our personal well-being enables us to contribute to our family, to our community, and to the world. We need only look around us to see many examples of people who are doing much to benefit others, yet still find time to take care of themselves.

As we noted at the beginning of this book, CLUES asks its clients, "What are your hopes and dreams for your future?" "Doing good for the family" appears at some point in most of their answers. In this book, we hope we have helped you learn about the many ways you can improve your personal well-being so that you can benefit your family and, ultimately, your community. Identity, family, emotions, attitudes toward alcohol and other drugs, financial knowledge, immigration experience, and spirituality are all components of personal well-being. As we grasp these features of our life, we can become better at realizing our hopes and dreams.

We are confident that, like many others, you will find that as you nurture your personal well-being, the well-being of your family will blossom.

# Search Institute's Framework of Developmental Assets for Adolescents
## (Ages 12 to 18)

This publication presents research on developmental assets, which are positive factors in young people, families, communities, schools, and other settings that have been found to be important in promoting young people's healthy development. Further details on developmental assets are available at www.search-institute.org/assets.

**External Assets**

*Support*

1. **Family support**—Family life provides high levels of love and support.

2. **Positive family communication**—Young person and her or his parent(s) communicate positively, and young person is willing to seek advice and counsel from parents.

3. **Other adult relationships**—Young person receives support from three or more nonparent adults.

4. **Caring neighborhood**—Young person experiences caring neighbors.

5. **Caring school climate**—School provides a caring, encouraging environment.

6. **Parent involvement in schooling**—Parent(s) are actively involved in helping young person succeed in school.

*Empowerment*

7. **Community values youth**—Young person perceives that adults in the community value youth.

8. **Youth as resources**—Young people are given useful roles in the community.

9. **Service to others**—Young person serves in the community one hour or more per week.

10. **Safety**—Young person feels safe at home, at school, and in the neighborhood.

*Boundaries and Expectations*

11. **Family boundaries**—Family has clear rules and consequences and monitors the young person's whereabouts.

12. **School boundaries**—School provides clear rules and consequences.

13. **Neighborhood boundaries**—Neighbors take responsibility for monitoring young people's behavior.

14. **Adult role models**—Parent(s) and other adults model positive, responsible behavior.

15. **Positive peer influence**—Young person's best friends model responsible behavior.

16. **High expectations**—Both parent(s) and teachers encourage the young person to do well.

*Constructive Use of Time*

17. **Creative activities**—Young person spends three or more hours per week in lessons or practice in music, theater, or other arts.

18. **Youth programs**—Young person spends three or more hours per week in sports, clubs, or organizations at school and/or in the community.

19. **Religious community**—Young person spends one or more hours per week in activities in a religious institution.

20. **Time at home**—Young person is out with friends "with nothing special to do" two or fewer nights per week.

**Internal Assets**

*Commitment to Learning*

21. **Achievement motivation**—Young person is motivated to do well in school.

22. **School engagement**—Young person is actively engaged in learning.

23. **Homework**—Young person reports doing at least one hour of homework every school day.

24. **Bonding to school**—Young person cares about her or his school.

25. **Reading for pleasure**—Young person reads for pleasure three or more hours per week.

*Positive Values*

26. **Caring**—Young person places high value on helping other people.

27. **Equality and social justice**—Young person places high value on promoting equality and reducing hunger and poverty.

28. **Integrity**—Young person acts on convictions and stands up for her or his beliefs.

29. **Honesty**—Young person "tells the truth even when it is not easy."

30. **Responsibility**—Young person accepts and takes personal responsibility.

31. **Restraint**—Young person believes it is important not to be sexually active or to use alcohol or other drugs.

*Social Competencies*

32. **Planning and decision making**—Young person knows how to plan ahead and make choices.

33. **Interpersonal competence**—Young person has empathy, sensitivity, and friendship skills.

34. **Cultural competence**—Young person has knowledge of and comfort with people of different cultural/racial/ethnic backgrounds.

35. **Resistance skills**—Young person can resist negative peer pressure and dangerous situations.

36. **Peaceful conflict resolution**—Young person seeks to resolve conflict nonviolently.

*Positive Identity*

37. **Personal power**—Young person feels he or she has control over "things that happen to me."

38. **Self-esteem**—Young person reports having a high self-esteem.

39. **Sense of purpose**—Young person reports that "my life has a purpose."

40. **Positive view of personal future**—Young person is optimistic about her or his personal future.

# Notes

1. From 2010 U.S. Census form definitions.

2. Maria Elena Ruiz and H. Edward Ransford, "Latino Elders Reframing *Familismo*: Implications for Health and Caregiving Support," *Journal of Cultural Diversity* 19, no. 2 (2012), 50–57.

3. Rory, "Latino Culture-*Personalismo*," CommonGround International, accessed February 1, 2013, http://commongroundinternational.com/personalismo-whats-your-approach.

4. Rosalyn Negro, "Respeto" in *Encyclopedia of Immigrant Health*, Sana Loue and Martha Sajatovic, eds. (New York: Springer Reference, 2012), 1295–6.

5. Pew Research Center, "Changing Faiths: Latinos and the Transformation of American Religion," (2007), 5.

6. Marta Tienda and Faith Mitchell, eds., *Hispanics and the Future of America* (Washington, DC: National Academies Press, 2006), 140.

7. Michelle Allen et al., "What Research Tells Us about Latino Parenting Practices and Their Relationship to Youth Sexual Behavior," (2008), 2.

8. "Developmental Milestones: 12 Months," American Academy of Pediatrics, last modified August 7, 2013, www.healthychildren.org/English/ages-stages/baby/pages/Developmental-Milestones-12-Months.aspx; "Infant Development: Milestones from 4–6 Months," Mayo Clinic, www.mayoclinic.com/health/infant-development/FL00099.

9. "Developmental Milestones: 2 Year Olds," American Academy of Pediatrics, last modified August 6, 2013, www.healthychildren.org/English/ages-stages/toddler/pages/Developmental-Milestones-2-Year-Olds.aspx.

10. "Developmental Milestones: 3–4 Year Olds," American Academy of Pediatrics, last modified July 9, 2013, www.healthychildren.org/English/ages-stages/preschool/pages/Developmental-Milestones-3-to-4-Year-Olds.aspx; "Developmental Milestones: 4 to 5 Year Olds," American Academy of Pediatrics, last modified July 9, 2013, www.healthy-children.org/English/ages-stages/preschool/pages/Developmental-Milestones-4-to-5-Year-Olds.aspx.

11. "Handout: Developmental Milestones," National Resource Center for Permanency and Family Connections, www.nrcpfc.org/ifcpc/module_1/Module1_Handout4_DevelopmentalMilestones.pdf.

12. Ibid.

13. Sheena Carter, "Alternatives to Physical Punishment," Emory University School of Medicine Department of Pediatrics, 2013, www.pediatrics.emory.edu/divisions /neonatology/dpc/alternat.html; "What About Punishment," American Academy of Pediatrics, last modified May 11, 2013, www.healthychildren.org/English/family-life /family-dynamics/communication-discipline/Pages/What-About-Punishment.aspx.

14. Adapted from Mayra A. Bamaca, "How Latino Parents Can Help Children Succeed in School," last modified May 17, 2010, www.education.com/reference/article /important-role-parents-latino-youth-succeed/.

15. Jessica Dennis, Tatiana Basañez, and Anahita Farahmand, "Intergenerational Conflicts among Latinos in Early Adulthood: Separating Values Conflicts with Parents from Acculturation Conflicts," *Hispanic Journal of Behavioral Sciences* 32, no. 1 (2010), 130-31.

16. Alexis O. Miranda et al., "Latino Families: The Relevance of the Connection Among Acculturation, Family Dynamics, and Health for Family Counseling Research and Practice," *The Family Journal: Counseling and Therapy for Couples and Families* 14, no. 3 (2006), 270.

17. Karla D. Wagner et al., "The Role of Acculturation, Parenting, and Family in Hispanic /Latino Adolescent Substance Use: Findings from a Qualitative Analysis," *Journal of Ethnicity in Substance Abuse* 7, no. 3 (2008), 304–27.

18. "Domestic Violence," U.S. Department of Justice, last modified March 2013, www .ovw.usdoj.gov/domviolence.htm.

19. "Understanding Intimate Partner Violence," National Center for Injury Prevention and Control, 2012, www.cdc.gov/ViolencePrevention/pdf/IPV_factsheet-a.pdf.

20. The National Domestic Violence Hotline, www.thehotline.org/is-this-abuse/information -for-immigrants/#1.

21. Sources include National Institute on Alcohol Abuse and Alcoholism, www.niaaa.nih .gov; and Craig Freudenrich, "How Alcohol Works," howstuffworks, http://science .howstuffworks.com/alcohol1.htm.

22. NYS Office of Alcoholism and Substance Abuse Services, *The Alcohol and Drug Primer*, www.oasas.ny.gov/admed/documents/AOD-PRIMER.pdf.

23. Kelsey Campion, CLUES chemical health counselor, "Chemical Dependency Counseling and the Hispanic/Latino Client," circa 2007.

24. Substance Abuse and Mental Health Services Administration, *Results from the 2010 National Survey on Drug Use and Health: Summary of National Findings*, (Rockville, MD: Substance Abuse and Mental Health Administration, 2011),www.samhsa.gov/data /NSDUH/2k10ResultsRev/NSDUHresultsRev2010.pdf.

25. "Frequently Asked Questions," Centers for Disease Control and Prevention, last modified July 2013,www.cdc.gov/alcohol/faqs.htm#alcoholismAbuse.

26. "Key Features of Risk and Protective Factors," Substance Abuse and Mental Health Services Administration, http://captus.samhsa.gov/prevention-practice/prevention -and-behavioral-health/key-features-risk-protective-factors/1.

27. Chart from Arturo Sesma Jr. and Eugene C. Roehlkepartain, "Unique Strengths, Shared Strengths: Developmental Assets among Youth of Color," *Search Institute Insights & Evidence*, 1, no. 2 (2003), 2.

28. "Hispanics: A People in Motion," Pew Research Hispanic Trends Project, last modified January 24, 2005, www.pewhispanic.org/2005/01/24/v-assimilation-and-attitudes.

29. Mark Hugo Lopez and Richard Fry, "Among Recent High School Grads, Hispanic College Enrollment Rate Surpasses That of Whites," Pew Research Center, last modified September 4, 2013, www.pewresearch.org/fact-tank/2013/09/04/hispanic -college-enrollment-rate-surpasses-whites-for-the-first-time.

30. "ESL Resources: FAQs," Center for Adult English Language Acquisition, www.cal.org /caela/esl_resources/faqs.html.

31. Julia Beckhusen et al., "Living and Working in Ethnic Enclaves: English Language Proficiency of Immigrants in U.S. Metropolitan Areas," *Papers in Regional Science* 92 (2013), 305–328.

32. Rights are from the section "Your Rights Regardless of Visa Status," in http://travel. state.gov/pdf/Pamphlet-Order.pdf.

33. "What Is 5-Year Cost to Own?" Kelley Blue Book, www.kbb.com/new-cars/total-cost -of-ownership/?r=43288880260661250.

34. Mark Schneider, "Higher Education Pays: But a Lot More for Some Graduates Than for Others," College Measures, September 3, 2013, http://collegemeasures.org/post/2013/09 /View-full-report-here.aspx.

35. Tatiana M.V. de Almeida, "American Sueño: Hispanic Immigrants' Cultural Adaptation in Small American Cities" (paper presented to the faculty of Liberty University School of Communication Studies, May 2012), 53, http://digitalcommons.liberty.edu/cgi /viewcontent.cgi?article=1222&context=masters.

36. Ibid., 27.

37. "U Visa for Immigrants Who Are Victims of Crimes," U.S. Immigration Support, www.usimmigrationsupport.org/visa-u.html.

38. Ana Gonzalez-Barrera and Jeffrey S. Passel, "An Awakened Giant: The Hispanic Electorate Is Likely to Double by 2030," Pew Research Hispanic Trends Project, last modified November 2012, www.pewhispanic.org/2012/11/14/an-awakened -giant-the-hispanic-electorate-is-likely-to-double-by-2030.

39. Pew Research Center, "Changing Faiths."

40. Ibid.

41. Maureen Campesino and Gary E. Schwartz, "Spirituality among Latinos/as: Implications of Culture in Conceptualization and Measurement," *Advances in Nursing Science* 29, no. 1 (2006), 69–81.

42. Ibid.

43. Ibid.

44. Ibid.

45. Pew Research Center, "Changing Faiths."

46. Ibid., 23–4.

47. Efren Maldonado, "Changing the Mission and Culture of a Congregation: A Case Study of a Latino Church," unpublished, 2012.

48. Pew Research Center, "Changing Faiths," 26.

# About the Authors and CLUES

Comunidades Latinas Unidas En Servicio

THIS BOOK WAS WRITTEN collaboratively by staff at the Twin Cities–based nonprofit Comunidades Latinas Unidas En Servicio, or CLUES, together with writer Vince Hyman. Its contributors include Karla Bachmann, Mauricio Cifuentes, Alejandro Valenzuela, Efren Maldonado, and Judy Cavazos-Beal.

With offices in St. Paul and Minneapolis, Minnesota, CLUES was established in 1981 by Latinos for Latinos. The original founders, who were mental health professionals, recognized that many Latinos faced cultural and linguistic barriers when accessing services. Since its inception, CLUES programs and services have connected families to resources, skills, institutions, and systems that create opportunities for self-sufficiency and empowerment. Its mission is to advance the capacity of Latino families to be healthy, prosperous, and engaged in their communities.

Today the agency serves over 10,000 people annually and focuses on family-centric services that impact health and family well-being (including mental and chemical health), educational achievement, economic vitality, and cultural and civic engagement.

CLUES Health and Family Well-being services focus on providing education, prevention, intervention services targeting the mind, body, and social well-being of clients. Services include mental and chemical health, family well-being, elder care and support, health navigation, and community health worker outreach. Economic Vitality services focus on helping clients strengthen their families and communities by reducing poverty through asset and prosperity building strategies such as financial coaching, workforce and career advancement, education and training, ESL and citizenship, and housing services.

Visit us at www.CLUES.org.